Praise for *Doxology*

The wide spectrum of voices heard in this book comes together to give an engaging and thorough look at the high calling the worship leader has in the local church. It expertly captures the marriage of passion and purpose, Christ-centeredness and mission, and spirit and truth to which the Scripture calls all worshippers of God.

Matt Carter, Pastor of Teaching and Vision,
Austin Stone Community Church

Doxology and Theology should be a "must read" for any pastoral staff and worship team. The truths of this book transcend music ministry and touch on the biblical lifestyle and worldview of any minister. Much of the teaching in this book I had to learn by trial and error. I wish I had this book twenty years ago.

Joel Engle, Lead Pastor, The Exchange Church

Doxology and Theology is filled with gospel truth and practical application for those who have the important task of lifting our hearts in song to the Triune God who in love has saved us. May this book equip church musicians, songwriters, and worship leaders to celebrate and savor the gospel of Jesus Christ!

Trevin Wax, Bible and Reference Publisher, B&H,
and author of *This Is Our Time* and
Gospel-Centered Teaching

I picked up the manuscript and could not put it down! It was one of the most engaging books I've read in a long time and on an area that isn't written on a whole lot—worship. The theology was very clear and engaging, but the practical application of that from how you live that out on a week-to-week basis is unsurpassed from anything I've ever read. This book should be read by every pastor, but especially every young pastor and church planter and should be kept close by as a reference and guide in the local church.

Bob Roberts Jr., Senior Pastor NorthWood Church
and author of *Bold as Love*

Instead of offering merely the nuts and bolts of worship leadership, the wise voices represented in this book provide a rich biblical foundation for the current worship leader to stand upon, unanimously raising the bar of leadership to its rightful place.

Justin Buzzard and Colin Dobrin, Lead Pastor and
Worship Leader, Garden City Church in Silicon
Valley

Standing favorably alongside Bob Kauflin's *Worship Matters*, this is another strategic volume full of sound theology as well as sound practical insights. The breadth and depth of this volume (and of its authors) is amazing. And, crucially, these men are all practitioners, active worship leaders themselves. "They know whereof they speak"! What an encouragement to see young leaders in our day taking this kind of stand for biblical faithfulness, spiritual integrity, and wholehearted engagement in worship (and in life). Worship leaders, and through them the churches they lead, will benefit tremendously from the wise and seasoned counsel found within these pages.

Ron Man, D.Min.
Director, Worship Resources International

Doxology and Theology is more than a book that is read once and then shelved. I believe the Lord will use *Doxology and Theology* of the true pastoral calling and stewardship of the worship leader as pastor and theologian. Matt Boswell has organized and edited a much-needed book that focuses on how the gospel shapes and informs every aspect of a worship leader's life. This is a must-read for anyone who leads and sculpts worship for the local church.

Dr. Joseph Crider, Senior Associate Dean of the
School of Church Ministries Division of Biblical
Worship, Southern Baptist Theological Seminary

God's Son fervently worshipped in spirit and truth brings down His glory at church. And that's what the church is all about, right? God's glory! That's why this book resonates so deeply with my heart. It is about vertical worship; giving God His rightful place in our corporate worship. I commend this great resource to every pastor, worship leader, and worshipper. May God alone get the glory He deserves.

Dr. James MacDonald, Senior Pastor, Harvest Bible
Chapel and author of *Vertical Church*

The calling and role of the worship leader in the life of the church have slowly degenerated in many circles of modern Christianity to being man-centered and performance-based. I am so grateful for the heart behind this book that seeks to bring clarity to the role of the worship leader by rooting it in the Word of God. This book calls for godly men who have personally been transformed by the gospel to lead the church in a proper response to the magnificent truths of the gospel. It challenges the worship of the church to be centered on God, focused on the grace of Jesus, and saturated by the Word of God. The writers of this book are men who speak from experience, having lived out this calling in their local church. I am elated about the potential of this book to raise up a generation of worship leaders who establish doxology on rich theology.

Afshin Ziafat, Lead Pastor,
Providence Church, Frisco, Texas

as a resource that worship leaders and worship teams continually turn to for refreshment, wisdom, and encouragement.

Eric Geiger, Senior Pastor, Mariners Church

I thank God for Matt Boswell's friendship and his commitment to scripturally governed, gospel-filled, Spirit empowered congregational worship. *Doxology and Theology* is the fruit of that commitment. Matt has brought together a thoughtful group of young (at least younger than me) theologian-musicians who will stretch and deepen your ideas of what it means to lead others in corporate worship. Most important, their thoughts will inspire a greater devotion and obedience to the Savior, who is worthy not only of our songs, but our lives.

Bob Kauflin, Director of Sovereign Grace Music,
author of *Worship Matters*

A provocative, comprehensive resource for gospel-centered worship—written by the leading voices in the new movement. Beyond fads and styles, this book anchors the weekend "worship experience" in theology and the overall missiology of the church. The fires of my soul were stoked as I read it. I am so excited about what God is doing in a rebirth of God-glorifying, disciple-making, mission-advancing worship. Enthusiastically recommended.

J.D. Greear, President, Southern Baptist
Convention; Lead Pastor, Summit Church, Raleigh-
Durham, North Carolina, author of *Stop Asking
Jesus Into Your Heart: How To Know For Sure You
Are Saved* and *Gospel: Recovering the Power That
Made Christianity Revolutionary*

For far too long worship leaders of all ages and in many different contexts have thought of themselves primarily as musicians and Christian artists. While those titles and roles have worked functionally, they have fallen woefully short

DOXOLOGY
& THEOLOGY

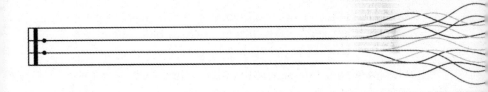

matt boswell

B&H
PUBLISHING GROUP
Nashville, Tennessee

Published by B&H Publishing Group

Nashville, Tennessee

Dewey Decimal Classification: 264

Subject Heading: Worship \ Public Worship \
Doctrinal Theology

6 7 8 9 10 11 12 • 23 22 21 20 19

Dedicated to the next generation.

CONTENTS

ACKNOWLEDGMENTS

Thank you to each of the authors of this book. You men have a deep love for the glory of Christ, and the good of His church. You each walk faithfully in light of the declaration of the gospel and call your churches to the same. I am deeply thankful that men like you are leading local congregations in the worship of our God.

Thank you to the lead pastors of each of our churches. Each of you men have influenced not only your worship leader, but all of the authors of this book in countless ways. Thank you for shepherding us and allowing us to shepherd alongside of you in the work of the ministry. Thank you also to each of the wonderful churches represented, for allowing your worship leaders to lead you and also influence others beyond your church.

Thank you Elliot Grudem and Mike Hall for planting this seed, and Josh Patterson for helping it grow. Thank you to our friends at LifeWay who have helped make this idea a reality: Eric Geiger for your leadership and Jedediah

Coppenger for seeing this book through to completion. Thank you also to Jennifer Grisham, Will Baker, Ron Man, and Kim Stanford for your editing contributions.

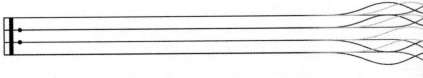

Introduction

Matt Boswell

God is raising up a generation of gospel-centered worship leaders. They desire to think theologically, not just pragmatically. They want to understand the fullness of the gathering of the church and the role of the worship leader, not just how to lead three verses and a chorus. Furthermore, pastors and churches alike increasingly express a desire to be led by thoughtful worship leaders who understand the life-changing marriage between doxology and theology.

Some may think that theology in the hands of worship leaders is not necessary in the course of their service to the church, but worship leaders are and must be practicing theologians. C. S. Lewis, in his masterpiece *Mere Christianity*, penned these words, which ring true decades later:

> Everyone has warned me not to tell you
> what I am going to tell you in this last book.
> They all say "the ordinary reader does not want
> Theology; give him plain practical religion."
> I have rejected their advice. I do not think the
> ordinary reader is such a fool. Theology means
> "the science of God," and I think any man who
> wants to think about God at all would like to
> have the clearest and most accurate ideas about
> Him which are available. You are not children:
> why should you be treated like children?[1]

Like Lewis, a growing army of worship leaders believes that theology is not just for the academics—it is for every Christian, especially worship leaders. Since worship leaders are those who lead the people of God in encountering Him in corporate worship, then above all things, we ought to study Him. Therefore, our first pursuit is not to lead worship, but to worship. And as we are set ablaze by God's truth, we become enabled to lead the people of God in life-transforming worship.

We pray that God uses this book to awaken your mind and your heart to the incredible role that worship leaders should play in the life of the mission of God.

About the Authors

Each of the authors selected for the chapters are faithful men who love the gospel of Christ, and are passionate about serving the local church in worship. They are also friends. God has graced each of them with hearts to serve, families to lead, and people to love. He has also entrusted them with a platform to teach and lead worship in various circles of influence. For the sake of this project, we have joined together to help raise our voice collectively in rethinking and reforming the role of the worship leader.

In editing, I have tried to maintain the unique voice of each author. Some chapters will assume a more conversational tone, and others will be more academic in nature. With each page, my prayer is that God would be glorified, and a new generation of worship leaders would be shaped by the Word of God.

For the glory of God and the joy of His church,
Matt

1

Reforming the Role of the Worship Leader

Matt Boswell, Providence Church (Frisco, Texas)

When I was fifteen years old I became a worship leader. Our youth pastor resigned his position at our church, which left us with no one to lead singing for our youth group. I learned to play some guitar chords and picked out a few simple songs. I had no formal training, little theological aptitude, and an overdose of immaturity, and I became a worship leader.

That time in recent church history was marked by transparency. Not the value of being transparent about trials and sin, but the clear pages of paper called transparencies by which churches projected song lyrics using an overhead projector. (Thankfully, this phase was brief.)

The church in America was rapidly changing its worship practices. The common piano/organ combination gave way to full bands. Drums were entering the musical landscape. (My apologies to everyone who had to endure the electronic drum kit.) Church hymnody was changing too. Hymnals were being replaced by projection software, which changed how we interacted with the practice of singing. Short, simple songs emerged that communicated plainly the work of God's redeeming grace (Vineyard Music, Maranatha), and focused heavily on the response of the worshipper. It was into this shifting church climate I set out on a journey of learning to lead worship.

The Winds of Change

Around this time the modern expression of the worship leader transformed. The role of church song leaders went through a serious overhaul led by modern songwriters who were influenced by the Christian music industry. In many churches the role of the music director changed from leading songs to leading worship.

Churches expected worship leaders to not only be musically gifted but also pastoral. Perhaps this is most clearly seen by the new job titles that were distributed. The person who was once called the "music minister" or "choir director" was now known as the "worship leader" or "worship pastor." This modification showed that a greater emphasis and responsibility was given to the person leading the singing in a church service.

Some of the ideas that swept through church music departments brought significant challenges, deemed the "worship wars." Unfortunately, some of these changes escalated into battles over musical style, which type of songs were being sung, and personal preference. In some cases tradition was abandoned in a move of sheer iconoclasm, while other churches split altogether over their worship practices. But God worked through the wars to bring about new life.

Today, many churches enjoy a new freedom and gospel clarity that was not always present in the past. Congregations are being led in song, prayer, and praise by worship pastors who are musically excellent, theologically equipped, and pastorally called. New hymns are being written that are filled with articulate doctrine and stirring melodies. Nothing is perfect or finished, but we have good reasons to celebrate.

The role of the worship leader went through its own reformation, but the work is not done.

Always Reforming

As worship leaders, we must always be reforming. We must continue to hold our worship practices up to the light of God's Word to see where they need more clarity, revision, or correction. The phrase "always reforming" was birthed out of the Protestant Reformation, originating from the Latin phrase *semper reformanda*. Michael Horton explains the origin of the phrase: "The saying first appeared in 1674 in a devotional book by Jodocus van Lodenstein. It is important to see the entirety of van Lodenstein's phrase: *ecclesia reformata, semper reformanda secundum verbi Dei.*" Translated: "The church is reformed and always in need of being reformed according to the Word of God." Horton continues, "The motto of our practices of worship must not be 'forward' but 'backward' to the Scripture."[1] This describes the important work and trajectory of the modern worship leader: always back to Scripture.

We are praying for a generation of worship leaders who are committed to this work of always reforming our practices to the Word of God. We want to think rightly in our doctrine of God and feel deeply in our worship of God. We've called this book *Doxology and Theology* because of the inter-play of these two ideas: biblical thinking and extravagant worship. The foundation of doxology is theology, and the goal of theology is doxology. This chapter will look at the importance of always reforming the worship leader's mind and heart according to the Word of God.

Reforming Our Minds

Worship leaders are singing theologians. We communicate truth with poetry and verse; we organize doctrine with rhythm and rhyme; we proclaim the good news through melody and harmony. With every stanza of every hymn, we are articulating and teaching what we believe, intentional or not. Because of this, worship leaders must be careful thinkers. We must pray for and work toward the continual reforming of our minds.

The commitment to be a worship leader is a commitment to theological growth. Words like *theology* should not intimi-date us because we are musicians. If the "worship wars" of the 1990s revealed anything, it is that the thing our churches need most from "worship leaders" or "music ministers" (whatever your title) is a robust and growing understanding of theology. Theology should inspire us to continued pursuit of God. As a matter of fact, the word *theology* is defined simply as the study of God, and I cannot think of a people who should be more committed to the study of God than those who lead others in worship. Worship leaders should lead God's people with both musical and theological skill, being continually reformed and renewed by the Word of God (Rom. 12:1).

Students of the Word

Reforming our minds begins with becoming students of the Word. The Bible must play a primary role in the spiritual formation of the worship leader. Psalm 119 poetically presents the Word of God as a treasure to be desired (119:72), a lamp that lights our path (119:11), as sweeter than honey (119:103). We are to read the Scriptures, meditate on them (119:15), cherish them (119:48), store them up (119:11), and pour them out of our lives (119:172). Jonathan Edwards understood how important the Word of God was to his growth in Christ. One of his resolutions was, "Resolved, to study the Scriptures so steadily, constantly and frequently, as that I may find, and plainly perceive myself to grow in the knowledge of the same."[2] We must resolve to grow as students of Scripture.

The Bible must also be the foundation of our worship practices. Christian worship is built upon, shaped by, and saturated with the Word of God. Scripture should inform our prayers, form our sermons, and transform our singing. Our services should not separate singing from the Word, but the church should hear the Word through singing.

Scripture and song are a tangled pair (Ps. 119:54). The most notable example of this is in the Psalms, as God's Word is given to be sung by his people. Other songs in Scripture, called canticles, appear outside the Psalms and also interweave poetry and praise (see Exod. 15:1–19; 1 Sam. 2:1–10; Luke 1:46–55; Luke 1:68–79).

Singers of the Truth

As a young worship leader I was not trained to think carefully through the songs we were singing. I sang what felt good, or what moved my emotions, with little attention paid to the diet of songs I was leading people in. I have stumbled through this journey, oftentimes crashing into innocent bystanders. I am so thankful for God's patience with me as I continue this journey of what it looks like to be a faithful singer of truth, leading people into singing and loving truth.

The primary task of the worship leader is to sing the truth. It is the commission of preachers to preach the truth, and the mandate of worship leaders to sing it. Albert Mohler noted, "Churches are looking for songs with no heresy. That is not enough."[3] We must take seriously the content of the songs we are singing, realizing how formative they are in the life of the church. Every word we sing ought to be weighed and measured for biblical faithfulness, theological weight, God-centeredness, singability, and effectiveness. There is no right praise without right doctrine.

The worship leader is often tasked with choosing the songs to be sung in church, so this should be done with great intentionality and care. Mark Dever and Paul Alexander give this advice to pastors and worship leaders: "As the main teaching pastor (or worship leader), it is your responsibility to shepherd the congregation into the green pastures of God-centered, gospel-centered songs, and away from the arid plains of theological vacuity, meditations on human experience, and emotional frenzy."[4]

The hymnal of the church has no back cover. Every church is in the process of curating its own collection of songs it will sing together in worshipping God. With this task comes the responsibility to carefully comb through an incredible (and ever expanding) body of hymnody and put forth the most truthful and beautiful songs we can find. While the task seems overwhelming, it doesn't have to be. Simply sing the truth, the whole truth, and nothing but the truth. (So help us, God.)

Thinking Carefully about Worship

Careful thinking is required of all people who lead worship. John Piper explains, "Thinking is one of the important ways that we put the fuel of knowledge on the fires of worship and service to the world."[5] Through the practice of careful thinking about God, His worship, His people, and His gospel, our churches will more fully experience happiness in Him!

This happiness is described in Psalm 1: "How happy is the one . . . [whose] delight is in the LORD's instruction, and he meditates on it day and night. He is like a tree planted beside flowing streams that bears its fruit in its season and whose leaf does not wither. Whatever he does prospers" (CSB). Thinking rightly about God by submitting to His Word leads to satisfaction in God, fruitfulness, and abundance in him.

There are also dangers to not thinking rightly about God, His Word, and how we worship Him. In recent years we've seen many worship leaders reject the authority of Scripture or fall into moral failure or both. One influential worship leader publicly changed his view on the historicity and inerrancy of Scripture. He now denies Christ's substitutionary death. Another worship leader professed her practice of homosexuality and embarked on a crusade to prove that her sin is biblically acceptable.

Both of these accounts fill my heart with sorrow: sorrow for the leaders, but moreso for the churches they served. These stories also serve as a warning to my own walk with

Christ. We each stand in need of the continual grace of God and must rely upon it completely. In our lives we will face varying temptations to doubt the Word of God, or to attempt to massage it to fit our whims and passion. We must practice thinking rightly about the Word of God in our lives and our churches.

Is your pursuit of becoming a better worship leader paired with becoming a better student of Scripture? When it comes to our lives and our worship practices, God's Word is the first and last word. We cannot worship God with our whole hearts if our minds are not also transformed by His truth. For us to respond rightly to God we must know and immerse our lives in His Word.

> *How firm a foundation, ye saints of the Lord,*
> *Is laid for your faith in his excellent word!*
> *What more can he say, than to you he hath said,*
> *You who unto Jesus for refuge hath fled?*[6]
> —George Keith, R. Keen (1787)

Reforming Our Hearts

Worship leaders must not only love God with our minds, but also with our hearts (Deut. 6:5). John Piper explains, "If we just know Him (God) in our minds, we're not doing anything different than the devil. The devil is one of the most theological, orthodox beings in the universe. He just hates what he knows about God."[7] It is not enough to allow truth to sit in our heads; it must rest in our hearts (Matt. 15:8). There is a grave difference between knowing about God and knowing God. Harold Best helps us understand the connection between thinking and feeling when he proposes, "We should strive for a thinking heart and a feeling mind."[8]

Over the years of leading worship, I have had to monitor my heart closely. At times I have done well, others I have not. My heart quickly grows rusty and clanky and needs the oil of the gospel to help work life back into it. Thomas Brooks warns about the need to mind our hearts when he says, "Most men's heads have outgrown their hearts."[9]

Some of us are wired more cognitively, others more emotionally. Some are thinkers. Some are feelers. Whether you find it easier to love God with your head or your heart, I'm praying that we will love God and lead His people with both truth-filled minds and burning hearts. May it never be said of us as worship leaders that our hearts have outgrown our heads, or our heads have outgrown our hearts.

The Heart of a Worshipper

Theology should make our hearts sing. If it doesn't, then something is missing the mark. Something is broken, and since the truth is never broken, the problem must be with our hearts themselves. The Bible shows us that we are born into sin, and are bent from the start to rebel against God.

Do you remember the first time you led people in singing? How sweet and fulfilling was it serving the people of God by aiming their gaze toward him? One of the challenges for worship leaders is to remember how sweet and simple this service is. The more time we spend doing anything, the more danger we're in to lose the sense of wonder and joy that God gives as we serve Him.

Imagine you are sitting in the waiting room for a doctor specializing in worship leaders. After flipping through last month's issue of *Golf Digest*, a nurse opens the door, calls your name, and leads you to a small examining room. A few minutes later, the doctor comes in and begins questioning the state of your heart. "Do you suffer from entitlement? Do you feel like you should be recognized more for your contributions to the church or praised for all you do? Are you discouraged as a worship leader? Are you frustrated by leading a small and 'under talented' group of musicians? Are you an apathetic worship leader? Have you withdrawn or judged the church rather than served it?"

If the diagnosis sounds like you, the doctor grabs the prescription pad and jots a short note. It simply says, "The gospel."

The beauty of the gospel is that we don't need to hide our sin. We are totally free to think through the state of our hearts—and our ministry—and confess our sins with full assurance that we can be forgiven. We are not welcomed by God because of our pure hearts, but because of Christ who was pure for us. The only heart received by God is the heart remade by the love of Christ. Our hearts were dead in sin, and they have been made alive in Christ (Eph. 2:5). And our hearts stand in need of continual attention. The heart of a worshipper is front and center in our practice of worship. As hymn writer Samuel Stone (1886) wrote,

> *Author of the new creation, giver of the second*
> *birth;*
> *May thy ceaseless renovations, cleanse our souls*
> *from stains of earth.*

Teaching and Admonishing

Paul acknowledges the important blending of truth and song as he writes to the church at Colossae: "Let the word of Christ dwell richly among you, in all wisdom teaching and admonishing one another through psalms, hymns, and spiritual songs, singing to God with gratitude in your hearts" (Col. 3:16 csb). Notice the practice of the Word dwelling among God's people while singing is happening. As the church sings, it teaches and encourages one another through the hymns they sing in a vital way. When a service is over and we scatter on mission, we carry with us the hymns we sang. They stick with us, instructing us and encouraging us. Charles H. Spurgeon elaborates,

> Paul thought that "Psalms and hymns and spiritual songs" were to be used for instruction and admonition as well as for the praises of God! And, to my mind, there is no teaching that is likely to be more useful than that which is accompanied by the right kind of singing! When I am preaching, I often find a verse of a hymn the very best thing I can quote—and I have not the shadow of a doubt that, frequently, a verse of sacred poetry has struck a man who has been altogether missed by the rest of the sermon.

I learned the importance of quoting hymns in sermons from Spurgeon, and can testify to the benefits I have seen from this practice. I have also experienced the benefit of leaving a service with the lyrics and melody of a hymn stirring my heart with love for Christ for days afterward. Songs are praise and adoration. Songs are teaching and exhorting. Songs are sermons.

Teaching through song requires leaders who are equipped for the work—both in music and Scripture. Worship leaders ought to lead the people of God with a guitar in one hand a

Bible in the other, and know how to use each weapon well. If Christian worship is built upon Scripture, then we cannot plan services if the Word of God does not play a primary role. If we are to teach and admonish one another through song, then the people choosing or writing the songs need to be well-versed in the emphasis, movement, and contours of the Bible. We must become singing theologians whose aim is to teach and proclaim the truth of God with accuracy and skillfulness.

It is possible to read Scripture regularly, to have orthodox worship services, to listen to expositional sermons week after week and still not cultivate love for God in our hearts. You can be completely right on paper and be completely wrong in your heart.

We should not be embarrassed at the thought of feeling deeply when we worship. We don't just pursue God with our minds, but also with our hearts. God's Word is meant to work through our emotions, to cause us to feel deeply, to love what we learn about God. There is a grave difference between knowing about God and knowing God.

When was the last time your theology made your heart sing? For some of us it may be that our theology isn't strong enough to make our hearts sing. Others of us may have hearts that have grown cold toward the working of the Holy Spirit.

We need both. We need minds washed with the water of the Word and hearts ablaze with the work of the Holy Spirit.

> *Prone to wander, Lord, I feel it, Prone to leave the*
>   *God I love;*
> *Here's my heart, O take and seal it; Seal it for Thy*
>   *courts above.*
> —Robert Robinson (1758)

Conclusion

It is not enough that our minds are filled with truth, but our hearts not filled with love. It is no use if our hearts are ablaze with passion, if our passions are not informed by truth. Our minds, hearts, and entire lives must find renewal in the power of the gospel, come under obedience to God, and be lived as worship to Him.

Skill may give a person a platform, but character will give them a voice. In order to be a leader in the local church, there are qualifications placed on our lives (1 Tim. 3; Titus 1). While worship leadership in local churches will look different from church to church, the people leading in song, in Scripture, and in prayer must be people whose lives are notably marked by a love for Jesus and love for others. Our worship must be holistic, touching every area of our lives.

What I am not saying is that there won't be times (perhaps many) where our lives are broken by sin or seasons where it seems temptation is winning the battle. In those seasons, we must practice repentance and run to the gospel, not run away from it. God will use unholy worship leaders in His divine providence, but His desire is for worshippers whose entire lives are marked with the fragrance with Christ.

I wish I could say that I have always walked in holiness as a worship leader. The truth is that in the early years of leading I hid unrepentant sin. I harbored unchecked pride. I was leading for a very large church, and writing songs that other churches began singing, but my spiritual life was neglected. While I was celebrated publicly (in very limited fashion), I was withering privately. I felt the sickness in my soul, but had difficulty dealing with it in the power of the gospel.

I knew that I needed help, perhaps a worship leader who could mentor and disciple me. I sent a letter (before e-mail was so accessible) to a well-known worship leader looking for guidance from someone who appeared to be doing what I felt called to. He never replied. Later, his secret drug addiction and repeated adultery were revealed. I find no joy in this man's fall. However, I share this story to show how vulnerable and dangerous it is to desire ministry, leadership, and more specifically worship leadership.

The modern adaptation of the worship leader is multifaceted, requiring careful thought and God's grace at every turn. This resource and our biennial conference exist because the needs and the challenges of the worship leader are continually changing. We must be "always reforming" our minds to the Word of God. We must be always reforming our hearts through the power of the Holy Spirit to grow in desiring, cherishing, and worshipping God. As a fellow traveler walking the same path toward the Celestial City, I encourage you: keep going. The work is worth the cost, and the joy that awaits us is worth the journey. May these following chapters help flesh out the life and labor the Lord has called you to as a worship leader.

> *Almighty author of my frame,*
> *To thee my vital pow'rs belong;*
> *Thy praise, (delightful, glorious theme!)*
> *Demands my heart, my life, my tongue.*[10]
> —Anne Steele (1760)

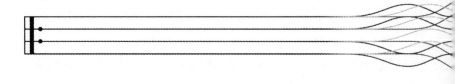

2

The Worship Leader and Scripture

Michael Bleecker, The Village Church (Lewisville, Texas)

Ethan stood in the pew directly in front of me. A high school student and new believer, he was passionate about many things, but celebrating the Lord through song topped his list. This Sunday morning was no exception. As the band began to play, the words of a beloved hymn shone on the screen and the church joined together singing:

> *All hail the power of Jesus' Name! Let angels prostrate fall.*[1]

We were eleven words in, and Ethan went from specta-
tor to participant. This was exciting to watch because I was
discipling him at the time, and the topic of worship had
been our focus. We spent time in John 4 that summer, dis-
cussing what Jesus meant when He said, "True worshipers
will worship the Father in spirit and truth" (John 4:23). We
defined words like *worship* and *glory*; we studied the difference between knowing and enjoying God. We learned what
physical expression looks like in the Bible, and talked about
our response when confronted with things like creation, salvation, providence, and majesty.

So, with his heart full and arms held high, Ethan belted
out the next line:

> *Bring forth the royal diadem and crown him*
> *Lord of all.*

Now, I usually don't spend time staring at other people
while I sing, but my desire to find teaching moments with
Ethan drove me to stare that morning. As we sang, I wondered if he knew what he was asking to be brought forth. I
wondered if he was lifting his hands because the truth of the
song stirred him, or if it was merely an emotional moment.
Hoping to reinforce what we studied that summer, I pulled
him aside after the service and asked if he knew what a
diadem was. He told me he didn't, so I spent the next few

minutes explaining that the "royal diadem" is a crown from Revelation 19:11 that Christ, the Word of God and the One called Faithful and True, will wear when He rides in victoriously on a white horse. I told him that all forces of evil would be defeated when the One whose eyes are like flames of fire rides in with "many diadems," and that the promise we've been given would be fulfilled when the diadem is brought forth and crowned on the King of kings and Lord of lords.

After that conversation, I thought about how much richer and sweeter that song would be to Ethan now, and how much richer and sweeter *all* our songs would be if we knew the truth in them.

This story, along with many others over the years, reinforced a devastating reality: Our churches are filled with uninformed worshippers.

Our Biblical Theology Should Inform and Propel Our Doxology

Where the Word of God is taught correctly, the opportunity exists for informed worshippers to respond to God with their heart *and* mind, with affection *and* thought. In John 4:23, Jesus tells the woman at the well what kind of worshippers the Father is looking for when He says, "True worshippers will worship the Father in spirit *and* truth" (emphasis added). The Word of God doesn't merely stir affections, but informs minds as well. "Truth without emotion produces dead orthodoxy and a church full (or half-full) of artificial admirers," John Piper writes. He continues,

> On the other hand, emotion without truth produces empty frenzy and cultivates shallow people who refuse the discipline of rigorous thought. But true worship comes from people who are deeply emotional and who love deep and sound doctrine. Strong affections for God rooted in truth are the bone and marrow of biblical worship.[2]

Our biblical theology (study of God) should inform and propel our doxology (praise to God).

Some of the richest theology in all of Scripture is found in Romans 1–11, culminating in the great hymn of Romans 11:33–36. Here, Paul teaches wonderful and weighty truths such as adoption, fulfilled promises, the gift of the Spirit, future glory, election, and eternal security to the Christian churches in Rome. The chapter ends with Paul breaking forth into praise:

> Oh, the depth of the riches and wisdom and
>   knowledge of God!
> How unsearchable are his judgments and how
>   inscrutable his ways!

"For who has known the mind of the Lord,
or who has been his counselor?"
"Or who has given a gift to him that he might
be repaid?"
For from him and through him and to him are
all things.
To him be glory forever. Amen. (Rom. 11:33–36)

Paul's rigorous study of the Word of God informed and propelled his doxology.

Similarly, we find Paul articulating the redemptive work of God in Christ to those in Ephesus. As I read Ephesians 3:14–20, I imagine Paul praying over the Gentiles with such fervor that they would know and savor the scope of God's breadth, length, height, and depth in Christ. In verse 21, his prayer turns into singing: ". . . to him be glory in the church and in Christ Jesus throughout all generations, forever and ever. Amen." The Truth that Paul knew and proclaimed pushed itself out into praise. Theology birthed a doxological response.

Just like those in the churches in Rome and Ephesus, those in our churches *should* be personally pursuing a richer biblical theology by eagerly "examining the Scriptures daily" (Acts 17:11), but that doesn't mean they *are*. As worship leaders and servants of Christ Jesus, we have been given the great responsibility to command and teach the things we have been trained in—"the words of the faith and of the good doctrine" (1 Tim. 4:6) and to delight in the law of the Lord, meditating on it "day and night" (Ps. 1:2). As we make preparations each week, we should remember, "Scripture is breathed out by God and profitable for teaching, for reproof, for correction, and for training in righteousness" (2 Tim. 3:16). Sadly, some are led each week by worship leaders who care more about the sound of the music than the weight of the truth. These are worship leaders who are uninformed and, at times, indifferent to the living and active Word of God that is "sharper than any two-edged sword, piercing to the division of soul and of spirit" (Heb. 4:12). The church cannot afford to settle for worship leaders who are capable musicians but are incompetent theologians.

Even after a couple of years at The Village Church, there were certain words and phrases in the songs I led that I didn't understand and, if asked, couldn't find in Scripture. I was simply regurgitating words without knowing if they were proclaiming truth. I realized my desperate need to study when someone asked me after singing "Come Thou Fount" if I knew what *Ebenezer* meant.

My first thought was of an old, grumpy man.

I was excited to find the word in 1 Samuel 7:12[3] and to learn that it is a "stone of help" (*Eben* is Hebrew for "stone" and *ezer* is Hebrew for "help"), erected to remind Israel of

God's faithfulness to help and restore them. Now when I sing, "Here I raise my Ebenezer, here by Thy great help I'm come," there is great weight to words that were once empty. As a teaching tool for our church, and to ground them biblically and theologically in what we are singing, I often put Scripture at the bottom of the slides. For "Come Thou Fount," I put 1 Samuel 7:12 at the bottom of that specific slide, along with a definition of *interposed* at the end of verse 2 and *fetter* in verse 3. The slides aren't as "clean" as they were before, but it's a great trade for informed worshippers.

If "Before the Throne of God Above" is in your rotation, have you thought to put Isaiah 49:16 at the bottom of your screen while you and your people sing, "My name is graven on His hands"?[4] Teach the Bible in your lyrics. Right theology will spill over into rich doxology.

What about words we say and sing all the time like *hallelujah, mercy, glory, justified, amen,* or even *worship*? Can you give someone a biblical definition for these words? Do you know that *Hosanna* stopped being a cry for help (Ps. 118:25) and became a shout of hope and exultation in recognition of Jesus as our Messiah in Matthew 21? And if you know this, do you teach it to your people and ask them to shout when they sing it as they're reminded of the hope, joy, and salvation that has come?

How different would the worship of our people be if we mined the depths of God's Word and taught it to our people? How rich would our worship be if the Word of God propelled it? What if our people actually understood what the words meant on our screens, in our songs, prayers, and teaching moments? How much richer would it be to use the word *glory* in these moments and know that it is the public display of the infinite beauty and worth of God? Or what if, before singing the word *hallelujah*, you taught your people that what they are about to sing is a word that translates to a joyous praise of boasting in the Lord?

Oh, that our churches would be filled with biblically informed people and theologically sound worshippers.

Thirty Minutes

Many evangelical churches devote around thirty minutes each weekend to a time of congregational singing. During this time, we're given the sacred trust of communicating to those in our churches the glory of Christ through song and spoken word. We are called to plead with our people to remember and behold Him, while imploring others to repent and be saved by Him. We are, of course, called to do this daily, not just in our short time each weekend. But you, worship leader, have this great opportunity to struggle for others, who willingly put themselves under your teaching each weekend, in the hope that their hearts would be encouraged and that they would "reach all the riches of full assurance of understanding and the knowledge of God's mystery, which is Christ" (Col. 2:2). How are you using your thirty minutes?

In Acts 8, Philip hears an Ethiopian eunuch reading Isaiah 53:7–8 aloud and asks him, "'Do you understand what you are reading?' And he said, 'How can I, unless someone guides me?'" (vv. 30–31). The eunuch invites Philip to sit with him, explains the Scriptures to him, and ultimately baptizes him. He used the time that he had to bring clarity to the Scriptures. We see that the eunuch, in verse 39, "went on his way rejoicing." His biblical theology informed and propelled his doxology.

The worship of those you are leading *will* be richer if you teach them the riches of the One they're celebrating.

Am I saying that those with little theological framework can't bring a pleasing offering to God? No, but just because it's okay for a child to play contently in a kiddie pool doesn't mean it's okay for an adult to play there also. In fact, it would be strange to see an adult doing this, wouldn't it? An adult should be discontent with the confines of a kiddie pool when there is deep water available. It's like gazing into the night sky and seeing only small lights dotting the darkness, as opposed to seeing innumerable spheres of gas illuminated by the Lord (Jer. 31:35) and held together by gravity in a galaxy surrounded by innumerable galaxies. Some look with deficiency upon a rainbow and see only bands of color refracting light, while others see bands of color representing a covenant (Gen. 9:13). Many people never make the connection that a covenant-keeping Creator has positioned these things in the sky for His glory. In the same way, many sing songs and hear words that are meaningless to them because they haven't been informed about what they're singing or hearing. The role of the worship leader is to equip and lead the church into deeper waters, so they may grow into greater levels of maturity.

And the deep water *is* available. Psalm 119 tells us that those who go into the deep waters are there because they're walking in His ways—in the law of the Lord. We can enjoy the depths of all God has for us if we fix our eyes on the Lord's commandments, meditate on His commands, and hide His Word in our hearts.

Still, some leaders neglect to teach the Bible every week. Perhaps they hope not to offend their hearers or maybe they have forgotten that they're to be devoted "to the public reading of Scripture, to exhortation, to teaching" (1 Tim. 4:13). The neglect is devastating when we remember that the Word of God . . .

- reveals "the glory of the LORD" (Isa. 40:5).
- "is a lamp to my feet and a light to my path" (Ps. 119:105).

- "is living and active, sharper than any two-edged sword, piercing to the division of soul and of spirit, of joints and marrow, and discerning the thoughts and intentions of the heart" (Heb. 4:12).
- keeps us from sinning (Ps. 119:11).
- is at work in believers (1 Thess. 2:13).
- is "the sword of the Spirit" (Eph. 6:17).
- makes one "wise for salvation through faith in Christ Jesus" (2 Tim. 3:15).
- "is breathed out by God and profitable for teaching, for reproof, for correction, and for training in righteousness" (2 Tim. 3:16).
- makes the man of God "complete, equipped for every good work" (2 Tim. 3:17).
- stands forever (Isa. 40:8).

A deficient view of the Word of God results in a deficient view of God. Do not neglect teaching it to your hearers, or showing it.

Propelled Doxology

Our biblical theology should inform *and* propel our doxology. What does doxology in motion look like? How do we outwardly demonstrate in worship what is inwardly taking place in the heart?

The two most prominent words for *worship* in the Bible are *histahawah* (HISt-a-ha-wah) in Hebrew and *proskuneō* (pros-koo-neh'-o) in Greek. Both of these words suggest the idea of bending over at the waist or physically falling down, as in reverence to a king. We are called to love God with our minds, hearts, and bodies (Deut. 6:5). We aren't disembodied spirits; so God intends that we use our whole beings to bring Him praise. Psalm 16:9 says, "My heart is glad, and my whole being rejoices; my flesh also dwells secure." And in Psalm 34:4–5, David proclaims, "Those who look to him are radiant, and their faces shall never be ashamed." Even our faces radiate a response when we look to the One who has delivered us. Knowing the riches of God should fuel our affections for Him. When it doesn't, one is subject to lifeless orthodoxy and legalism. When affections untethered to the truth arise, one is left, not walking in the truths He has ordained for us, but rather swimming in a sea of feelings about God. The result of this is sensationalism. Neither response leads to gospel-centered worship.

Our affections are tied to our understanding. Expressions of emotion about things we don't know are useless. Lifting one's hands in worship avails nothing if it is not in response to truth. One could easily fabricate physical expressions in worship while living in sin. God is not deceived by such showmanship: "When you spread out your hands, I will hide my eyes from you; even though you make many prayers, I will not listen; your hands are full of blood" (Isa. 1:15). Physical expressions of affection toward God, however, should result from rich moments with God. They are both commanded and spontaneously modeled in Scripture as a way of giving God glory.[5] Some of those ways include, but are not limited to:

- singing (Ps. 9:2)
- standing (Isa. 29:23)
- shouting (Ps. 71:23)
- praying (Ps. 5:3)
- dancing (Pss. 30:11; 149:3)
- sitting (2 Sam. 7:18)
- clapping (Ps. 47:1)
- laying prostrate (Matt. 26:39)
- lifting hands (Ps. 134:2)
- bowing low (Exod. 34:8)

We should be worshippers who know richly, feel deeply, and express passionately. My hope and challenge for you is that you will savor the supremacy of the Scriptures both in your personal life and in your corporate gatherings. It's time for us to feel the weight of our calling, and with humility and passion, lead those whom God puts in front of us each week.

Are you leading from a posture of humility? Are you marked as someone who has been transformed by the gospel? Are you leading from a place of believing in the sufficiency of Scripture? The Word of God is inerrant, infallible, and certain. It is the sole authority on all matters of faith and life and practice. As worship leaders, this includes the Scriptures forming the entirety of our lives from the private worship of our homes to the public worship of our congregations.

I leave you with a prayer by John Piper:

> The life-giving [worship leader] is a man
> of God, whose heart is ever athirst for God,
> whose soul is ever following hard after God,
> whose eye is single to God, and in whom by the
> power of God's Spirit the flesh and the world
> have been crucified and his ministry is like the
> generous flood of a life-giving river. . . .
>
> God, deliver us from the professionalizers!
> Deliver us from the low, managing, contriving,
> maneuvering temper of mind among us. God,
> give us tears for our sins. Forgive us for being
> so shallow in prayer, so thin in our grasp of
> holy verities [truths], so content amid perishing
> neighbors, so empty of passion and earnestness
> in all our conversation. Restore to us the child-
> like joy of our salvation. Frighten us with the
> awesome holiness and power of Him who can

cast both soul and body into hell. Cause us to hold to the cross with fear and trembling as our hope-filled and offensive tree of life. Grant us nothing, absolutely nothing, the way the world views it. May Christ be all in all.

Banish professionalism from our midst, Oh God, and in its place put passionate prayer, poverty of spirit, hunger for God, rigorous study of holy things, white-hot devotion to Jesus Christ, utter indifference to all material gain, and unremitting labor to rescue the perishing, perfect the saints, and glorify our sovereign Lord.

Humble us, O God, under Your mighty hand, and let us rise, not as professionals, but as witnesses and partakers of the sufferings of Christ.

In His awesome name. Amen.[6]

May our work remain fruitful, empowered by the Holy Spirit and saturated with truth—never shrinking from declaring the whole counsel of God (Acts 20:27).

3

The Worship Leader and the Trinity

Zac Hicks, Cathedral Church of the Advent (Birmingham, Alabama)

> *The proper study of God's elect is God; the proper study of a Christian is the Godhead. The highest science, the loftiest speculation, the mightiest philosophy, which can ever engage the attention of a child of God, is the name, the nature, the person, the work, the doings, and the existence of the Great God whom he calls Father.*
> —Charles Spurgeon

If we're honest, we're probably a little afraid to touch the doctrine of the Trinity. First of all, it's confusing and paradoxical. Second of all, throughout church history it appears to us that folks who spent too much time thinking about it ended up in heretical hot water. Ironically, while the Trinity Himself should engender a healthy fear in us, it is the *doctrine* of the Trinity that more often has us trembling.

Worship inevitably takes the shape of its object. Tribal animistic religions, where worshippers believe that the elements of the earth (plants, animals, weather patterns) are "animated" by spirits, are often characterized by a very earthy and physical worship. Buddhist monks worship in a slow, lengthy, meditative fashion because that is the shape of Nirvana's serenity. Ancient Greco-Romans adopted prostitution as a "sacred act" precisely because Aphrodite was the goddess of love and fertility. We who worship the one true and living God recognize that our worship should take *His* shape. And our God is Triune—Father, Son, and Holy Spirit—one God, eternally existing in three Persons.

Many in recent years have commented on the anemic state of much of evangelical worship in the twenty-first century. We are me-focused, a-theological, biblically illiterate, and entertainment-saturated, they say. Many of these critics offer a prescription for recovery, ranging from things as practical as a reform of liturgy or musical styles to things as philosophical as media ecology and aesthetics. I'm convinced, though, that many of these (important) observations find resolution when we begin to be more intentional as worshippers, worship planners, and worship leaders about allowing our worship to take the shape of our beloved Object. Worship shaped *by* the Trinity will inevitably take the form *of* the Trinity.

What Does Trinitarian Worship Look Like?

How does the reality that our God is Father, Son, and Holy Spirit affect what we do and how we do it? Let's look at four results that flow out of worship shaped by the Trinity.

The Trinity affects the possibility and proximity of worship.

The Trinity makes our worship possible. Sometimes discussions about worship too quickly gloss over the important fact that our worship of God is only made possible by God Himself, and that this possibility was affected by a decidedly Trinitarian action. When God was in the process of redeeming Israel from Egypt's bondage, the refrain repeatedly resounded that the reason for the redemption of the people of God was so that they would worship Him (Exod. 3:12, 18; 5:1, 3, 8; 7:16; 8:1, 20, 25–29; 9:1, 13; 10:3, 7–11, 24–27). God saves us *for* worship. But this salvation is not a random, haphazard occurrence; it is a well-calculated plan, masterfully engineered and executed by the Magnificent Three. The Father came up with the plan:

> Blessed be the God and Father of our Lord Jesus Christ, who has blessed us in Christ with every spiritual blessing in the heavenly places, even as he chose us in him before the foundation of the world, that we should be holy and blameless before him. In love he predestined us for adoption as sons through Jesus Christ, according to the purpose of his will, to the praise of his glorious grace, with which he has blessed us in the Beloved. (Eph. 1:3–6)

The Son, "for the joy that was set before him" (Heb. 12:2), accepted the marching orders of the Father and accomplished the mission given Him:

> Though he was in the form of God, [he] did not count equality with God a thing to be grasped, but emptied himself, by taking the form of a servant, being born in the likeness of men. And being found in human form, he humbled himself by becoming obedient to the point of death, even death on a cross. (Phil. 2:6–8)

The Holy Spirit then takes the finished work of the Son and applies it to believers, sealing it to us and sanctifying us by His very indwelling presence:

> You were washed, you were sanctified, you were justified in the name of the Lord Jesus Christ and by the Spirit of our God. (1 Cor. 6:11)

So, because the end of our salvation is worship, and because salvation is only made possible by the cooperative teamwork of the three Persons, it is only right to say that the Trinity is the reason our worship is even possible. Without the Father, Son, and Holy Spirit, we would be dead in our sin (Eph. 2:1–2; Rom. 3:10–18), unable to recognize God, much less worship Him.

However, the complete truth is even more profound than this. Not only has the Trinity saved us *to* worship, He has completed and perfected worship *for* us so that our worship might be acceptable. We often forget that it is not only Jesus' death that is applied to us by the Spirit, but His life, as well. Where we fail miserably in our feeble attempts at worship, Jesus succeeded fully. The perfect worship that the Father demands has found all its qualifications met in the Son's righteous living—both His personal piety and His fully obedient participation in corporate worship—while on earth. By the power of the Spirit, we are united with the Son, clothed in His righteous worship, such that the Father sees *His* worship as *we* worship. Jesus worships *for us!*[1] This should make "worship leaders" pause every time they assume that title. There is only one true Worship Leader, and His name is Jesus Christ (Heb. 9:11–15; 10:11–14). Trinitarian worship, then, at its core, is *the worship of the Father, through the Son, by the power of the Holy Spirit.* That said, should we then only directly worship the Father and not all three Persons? Not at all. If anything, the above statement is meant to show the Trinitarian direction and shape of worship by highlighting each of the Persons' roles. Scripture (e.g., Rev. 4–5),[2] our common creeds (e.g., the Nicene Creed), and some historic songs of the church (e.g., Gloria Patri, "Doxology") encourage direct adoration of Father, Son, and Holy Ghost. Robustly Trinitarian worship will therefore encapsulate both the "directional/role" aspect (*of* the Father, *through* the Son, *by* the Spirit) and the intentional praise of each Person.

One other question hangs over us: Is the notion we hear often of "Christ-centered worship" anti-Trinitarian because it highlights one Person over the others? Hopefully the answer, based on the discussion above, is a bit more self-evident. Christ-centered worship is Trinitarian worship because Christ is our access point to the Godhead (John 10:7, 9; 14:9). If we want to worship the Trinity and worship

"Trinitarian-ly," we can only do so *through the Son* (more on this below in the discussion of worship's gospel-shape).[3]

The Trinity puts us in close proximity to God. As we worship God, just how close are we to Him? The work of the Trinity helps us realize that we stand exceedingly near. The Spirit has sealed in believers not a side-by-side *tethering to* Christ but an interwoven *union in* Christ (Rom. 6:3–4). Believers don't worship at a distance, far removed from the Godhead. On the contrary, we find ourselves, in Christ, right in the middle of the Trinitarian Persons' mutual delight and self-giving. Scripture speaks of our somehow truly and really being in the very Holy of Holies, God's throne room, as we are "seated with him [Christ] in the heavenly places" (Eph. 2:6). Our union with Christ through the Spirit helps us make sense of Peter's statement of our shockingly close proximity to God: "He has granted to us his precious and very great promises, so that through them you may become partakers of the divine nature" (2 Pet. 1:4).[4]

The Trinity protects the priority and purity of worship.

The Trinity makes corporate worship a priority. Evangelicalism over the years has championed the cause of individual worship and piety. Evangelicals rightly emphasize the need for a personal relationship with God, and out of that emphasis flows a strong commitment to fostering individual devotional practice. An unintended consequence of this emphasis has been minimizing the value of corporate public worship. The Trinity helps correct this imbalance. If our one God truly is a Community of Persons, then true Christian worship is, at its core, inherently communal and corporate. The Trinitarian essence is multi-personal, and worship shaped like the Trinity should also be multi-personal. This doesn't minimize the need for our individual communion with Father, Son, and Holy Spirit. In fact, corporate worship and personal worship share a cyclical, symbiotic relationship.[5] Nevertheless, if God exists as a community, then the core of our faith, too, is expressed not as individuals, but as a church body. And if this is true, then corporate worship is one of the most fundamental elements of our faith. The Trinity makes corporate worship more than important. The Trinity makes corporate worship preeminent.

The Trinity preserves worship's purity. Several observers have noted the Trinity's conspicuous absence in much of the most popular worship songs of modern evangelicalism, some even proposing that our worship may be guilty of being "functionally Unitarian."[6] We often don't realize just how much our day-to-day spirituality is shaped by corporate worship. We sometimes strain to see that the way we worship shapes our desires and habits, much like the way we eat shapes our waistline. If the Trinity is conspicuously absent from our worship, not only are we *not* being shaped in a Trinitarian fashion, but we are being malformed into something impure, sub-Christian, even un-Christian.

Think, for instance, how de-Trinitized worship can lead to a Pelagian construct of our effort in worship.[7] Pelagius held to the notion that human beings aren't marred by original sin and don't need God to perform good works. This view, vigorously opposed by Augustine and others, was denounced as heresy in the fifth century. When the Trinity is hidden in our worship, it's much easier to forget about the Father's accepting the meritorious work of the Son in us by the power of the Spirit. Our hearts, being prone to wander, can easily slip into a self-inflated triumphalism ("God, *I'm* living for You," "*I'm* giving my all for You," etc.), feeling good about our worship, commitment, and effort. While claiming orthodoxy, we approach God in worship as functional Pelagians, convinced of the false notion that God is pleased with *our* worship, and suddenly we find our doxology and theology worlds apart. Heavy doses of Trinitarianism boil such impurities to the surface, and we are enabled to then name them for what they are and slough them off before they infect us like cancer.[8]

The Trinity affects the posture and procedure of worship.

The Trinity encourages a peaceful, humble posture. When our worship is shaped by the Trinity, our posture becomes one of peace and humility. We are at peace because, in worship, through Christ's finished work, our worship is not striving. Because the Spirit has applied the perfect worship of the Son to us, we're free to worship as ones delighting in God's glory rather than ones seeking to earn it. One intercessor, the Son, kneels before the throne of the Father, continually pleading the merit of His blood for us (Heb. 9:12; Rom. 8:34). The other intercessor, the Holy Spirit, prays to the Father all that we can't pray because we don't know how (Rom. 8:26–27). Because of the Trinitarian intercession, it takes all the pressure off us to "perform to please." Instead, we can "respond to delight."

The Trinity demands a humble posture as well. Because worship is only *through the Son*, it is decidedly a gift. The Father gives us the Son's worship through the Spirit. So, even as we believe that our worship is a response to God, the Trinity helps us see that it is, in the words of Matt Redman, a "gifted response."[9] Even, then, as our worship is joyous, the Trinity demands that it not be a pompous bravado full of triumphal claims about what we do for God. Our joy, though exuberant and expressive, can never be arrogant, because worship is a gift, neatly wrapped and delivered by Father, Son, and Holy Spirit.

The Trinity shapes how worship proceeds. If the Trinity truly is the initiator of worship and giver of worship's response, then the procedure of our worship will take a dialogical shape. In other words, a Trinity-shaped worship service will look like a back-and-forth conversation: God speaks, we respond, God speaks, we respond, and so on. Worship elements that can highlight our dialogue with the Trinity are things like:

- Call to Worship—a passage of Scripture that articulates the voice of God's summons to worship Him (e.g., Ps. 95);

- Confession of Sin—spoken or sung, an opportunity for us to respond to encountering God in all His holy splendor, rightfully crying, "Woe is me!" (Isa. 6:5);

- Assurance of Pardon—the Father's declaration of our pardon through the Son, either through a gospel-oriented song or a scriptural declaration of forgiveness in Christ;

- Sermon and Offering—God's preached Word to us, and our response of committing, consecrating, and giving ourselves to Him; and

- Benediction—a final word of blessing at the end of a service (God gets the last word), so that we are sent forth in the love, grace, and peace of God to share in God's mission in the world (e.g., Num. 6:24–26).

Trinitarian worship is not only naturally dialogical; it is also instinctively gospel-shaped. The gospel, because it is the good news that we share in the Trinitarian life with the Father, through the Son, and by the Spirit,[10] becomes the path on which a Trinitarian worship service proceeds. In worship, when we "rehearse" the gospel—God's holiness, our depravity and inadequacy, God's provision of Christ to bridge the divide (especially in the preached Word and at the Lord's Supper table), and our "gifted response" of offering ourselves through the power of the Spirit—we, in the words of the hymn attributed to St. Patrick, "bind unto ourselves the strong name of the Trinity." Gospel-shaped worship is inherently and robustly Trinitarian.[11]

Trinitarian shape extends even beyond individual Sundays, though. The entire year can follow the contour of the three Persons. Trinitarian shape is one of the reasons why an increasing number of churches appear to be returning to the traditional church calendar, for within a year, Christians walk through the foreordained plan of the Father (Advent), the arrival, ministry, and Passion of the Son (Christmas,

Epiphany, Lent, and Easter), and the abiding presence of the Spirit in the church (Pentecost). Both weekly and annually, then, we can abide in "Trinitarian balance."

The Trinity directs the practices and propositions of worship.

The Trinity should be reflected in our worship practices. The Trinity affects not only the structure of worship but also how we engage in it. For instance, we've noted that the Trinity's communal essence informs the priority of corporate worship, but our practices, too, should be shaped in a communal fashion. When we sing *together* we reflect the Trinity—many disparate voices join together in harmonic oneness. Trinitarian reflection is prized when we value the corporate voice of the congregation over the sound of the musical instruments pumped at overly high decibels. When our architecture, furniture, and "accessories" reflect our communal and corporate nature, we reflect the Trinity. Think of, for instance, one long pew (or even an open floor) that "joins many into one" versus a row of individual chairs or armed theater seats. Compare rounded, communally oriented sanctuaries versus deep, narrow worship spaces. We reflect the Trinity in how we engage in baptism and the Lord's Supper by asking how we can make these practices more symbolically communal and less individualistic.

The Trinity shapes the propositions of our sermons, prayers, songs, and readings. Besides structure and shape, perhaps the most obvious place to engage the Trinity is in the actual words we use in our prayers, songs, and readings. True Trinitarian worship is mindful of the unique roles of each of the Persons and at times addresses Father, Son, and Holy Spirit in accordance with those roles. Because it is the Spirit who guides us into all truth (John 16:13), we rightly pray *to the Holy Spirit* when we prepare to hear the Word of God preached or read. Because we rightly approach the Father through the Son, our prayers are decidedly "in Jesus' name." When thanking God for His great salvation, it is a more than worthy exercise to address each of the Persons, thanking them for their specific roles in our redemption—the Father's foreordination and plan, the Son's accomplishment of the plan, and the Spirit's application of the plan. The inverse of this is our avoidance of "Trinitarian confusion" by wrongly attributing something to one Member that belongs to another. For instance, many have pointed out the (probably just lazy) prayer sometimes heard from the lips of leaders in worship, "Father, thank You for dying on the cross for our sins."[12] In our songs, we want material that not only mentions the Persons but even addresses them and praises them individually. This is why many Christian communities have found such value in the historic songs of the church like the "Gloria Patri" and the "Doxology," both of which are explicitly Trinitarian. Additionally, Trinitarian worship encourages us to regularly use the great creeds and statements of faith that help articulate and preserve this blessed theology. Historic creeds like the Apostles' Creed and the Nicene Creed paint the Trinitarian backdrop on which the scene of our worship is set.

Preaching reflects the Trinity when it is gospel-centered and Christ-centered. Through Christ, we have access to the Father by the Spirit—this is the essence of the gospel and therefore the ultimate message and "big idea" of the Bible. If this is so, then true expository preaching that seeks to exegete and apply the Scripture will always arrive at God's "authorial intent" of lifting up the gospel of Jesus. Christ will be preached from every text, and the gospel will be the core of every application. Moralism, self-help talks, and all variations of the prosperity gospel are, therefore, anti-Trinitarian preaching.[13]

The Trinity, having redeemed us for the end goal of glorifying Him, leaves no aspect of worship untouched. Everything from worship's possibility to its structure and elements should be shaped by our Triune God, molded into His likeness. Most important, though, *we* are shaped by the Trinity, thrice marked in our personal and corporate worship with this indelible imprint:

Glory be to the Father,
And to the Son,
And to the Holy Ghost;
As it was in the beginning,
Is now, and ever shall be:
World without end. Amen.

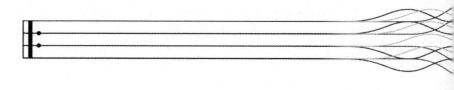

4

The Worship Leader and Mission

Matt Papa, Songwriter/Author/Worship Leader (Nashville, Tennessee)

"Let the peoples praise You, O God; Let all the peoples praise You. Let the nations be glad and sing for joy!"
—Psalm 67:3

"Missions exists because worship doesn't."
—John Piper

"Joy delights in joy."
—William Shakespeare

Introduction

The greatest injustice in the universe is not that there are people dying of AIDS or that people starving to death, even as you read this. It's not that there have been more than 50 million abortions in America since *Roe v. Wade*. It's not even that there are 27 million human slaves or 200 million orphans in the world today. These things are absolutely awful, and I believe they break God's heart. But these, even combined, are not the greatest injustice. *The greatest injustice in the universe is that there are human beings who do not worship Jesus Christ.*

God created humanity to worship and obey Him (Gen. 2:15; Col. 1:16), but we all have chosen to worship the creature rather than the Creator, who is forever praised (Rom. 1). This is injustice. God, infinitely holy and worthy of adoration, has been "set aside" (Rom. 4) by His quintessential creation as unsatisfying, unreliable, and at best useful.

This is suicide.

Humanity, through its disobedience, wandered from the fountain of all joy and life, the worship of God, and chose to drink from the poisonous puddle of idolatry. We have fallen short of God's glory (Rom. 3:23). In not doing what we were created to do, we have become, as C. S. Lewis so timelessly put it, "half-hearted creatures, fooling about with drink and sex and ambition when infinite joy is offered us" (Rom. 2).

We have "robbed" God of glory (Rom. 5) and ourselves of joy. This is injustice.

My aim is to show, in this chapter, how worship fuels missions (Rom. 3), and that missions rises and falls on the wings of worship. Christians and churches that are intensely doxological will be intensely missional, and those who fail to worship will fail to spread worship. Where are those who will fight so great an injustice? We must bid the nations to sing with us, for God's glory and their joy. The Lamb that was slain is worthy, and it is not enough for Him to be worshipped in America, in the comfort of our buildings. He is a Savior who must be worshipped everywhere.

The Nature of Joy, Singing, and Mission

I have always been fascinated with the fact that God commands us to *sing*. The Psalms are filled with commands like Psalm 47:6 which says, "Sing praises to God, sing praises! Sing praises to our King, sing praises!" Isn't that interesting? God could have just as easily made us creatures that could only speak, or creatures for whom He only desired communicative speaking. Yet, He calls us to *sing*. Why is this? It reminds me of the great commandment, where we are commanded to "love," which is equally interesting. Can love really be commanded? It's as if, throughout the pages of

Scripture, God is *commanding* our happiness. Commanding us to have joy. Love! Sing! Why does He do this?

I believe God does this because, in creating us to worship and enjoy Him, He knows that when we align ourselves with this purpose, our joy will be overflowing. And there is something about the nature of singing that illustrates joy more than anything else. We see this everywhere.

A father comes home after a long day of work, and excited to see his family, he bursts open the door singing "The Star-Spangled Banner" (or the first thing that pops into his mind). He is then dog-piled by his surprised, screaming children, which was his intention.

We see it in sports. Nearly every sports team that exists has some kind of victory-*song*.

We see it in Disney movies when two characters are so in love that words can no longer suffice to express the suppressed emotion of the moment, they *sing*.

Singing expresses our most deep-seated joys the way that crying does our sadness. When we are overwhelmed with joy, we sing! This is why God commands it. There is something so delightful—so ineffable—about God's numberless attributes, that it is not enough to simply verbally acknowledge them or write about them. We must sing! We must burst forth in adoration. C. S. Lewis speaks of this in his *Reflections on the Psalms*:

When I first began to draw near to belief
in God and even for some time after it had
been given to me, I found a stumbling block
in the demand so clamorously made by all
religious people that we should "praise" God;
still more in the suggestion that God Himself
demanded it. . . . But the most obvious fact
about praise—whether of God or anything—
strangely escaped me. I thought of it in terms of
compliment, approval, or the giving of honor. I
had never noticed that all enjoyment spontaneously overflows into praise. The world rings
with praise—lovers praising their mistresses,
readers their favorite poet, walkers praising
the countryside, players praising their favorite
game—praise of weather, wines, dishes, actors,
motors, horses, colleges . . . even sometimes pol-
iticians or scholars. I had not noticed how the
humblest, and at the same time most balanced
and capacious, minds, praised most, while the
cranks, misfits and malcontents praised least.
I think we delight to praise what we enjoy
because the praise not merely expresses but
completes the enjoyment; it is its appointed
consummation.[1]

We praise what we enjoy. We overflow. We sing; but that
is not all we do. Call me bold or foolish, but I will take Lewis

one step further in the discussion of the nature of joy. I don't think praise is *the* appointed consummation of joy, but *one of its* appointed consummations.

Something that I have learned about my wife over the years is that she is a food-sharer. There is never a time that we are eating when she does not say to me, in a childlike manner, "Try this!" I absolutely love this about my wife, but sometimes, this request puts me in a little predicament. If I don't want what she is offering me, what do I do? I chew, swallow, and smile. Most of the time, what she is offering is absolutely delicious, which is precisely the reason she wanted me to try it. *She enjoyed it, and wants me to share in her enjoyment.*

Now, I hope you are beginning to see the intricate relationship between worship and mission. Joy has one of its appointed consummations in *praising*, but it has another in *sharing*. What we find enjoyable we *naturally* find shareable, because joy shared is joy intensified. Shakespeare said it this way: "Joy delights in joy." We love to see others discover joy in the things we have discovered joy in, and our joy is increased when they praise what we share. We see this everywhere. When you hear a really funny joke, you call your best friend and laugh together. When you hear an incredible song, you post it to Facebook to let everyone hear it. When you take an adorable picture of your child, you send it to your extended family to get their "oh's" and "ah's." This is the way God created us, because this is the way God Himself is.

In "The End for Which God Created the World," Jonathan Edwards teaches that the Triune God, prior to creation, was completely satisfied in Himself: Father, Son, and Holy Spirit. God has never been lonely, and has always been happy. However, if the world had never been created, Edwards says that some of God's attributes, in some ways, "never would have had any exercise" (i.e., God's mercy, patience). Thus, it could be said that God's attributes were "pent-up" within Himself until the creation of the world when He overflowed with His own joy. Edwards describes it this way:

> As there is an infinite fullness of all possible
> good in God—a fullness of every perfection, of
> all excellency and beauty, and of infinite happi-
> ness—and as this fullness is capable of com-
> munication . . . so it seems a thing amiable and
> valuable in itself that this infinite fountain of
> good should *send forth* abundant streams.[2]

Thus, God created all things . . . similar to the way a songwriter creates a song. The songwriter doesn't need the song. The song is simply an overflow of who he is that "needs" to be communicated. God, in the creation of the world and humanity, sought to share His own joy with "a glorious society of created beings," in order to have His own joy increased. God loves to see us discover joy in the thing He is joyful in (His own glory), and His joy increases when we praise what He has shared. And diffusing any arguments that would show this to be a weakness in God, Edwards states simply, "It is no argument of the emptiness or deficiency of a fountain that it is inclined to overflow." *Joy shares joy.*

Worship as the Fuel of Missions

At pretty much every concert or conference that my band and I are a part of, I say this from the microphone at some point: "I believe with all my heart that God is going to use some of you in this room to turn the world upside down for Jesus [usually there is some small applause, and then I awkwardly interrupt it with this next statement]. But it's not because of you, how good you are, or how determined you are. It's simply because that's what happens when a human being sees God."

Throughout the Scriptures, when ordinary people see the majesty of God, or the mercy of God, they are forever changed by it, and they go tell everyone about it. That's just what happens. Moses encounters God at the burning bush, and then next thing you know he is prophesying to the most powerful man in the world, saying, "Let my people go!" (Exod. 8–11). The Samaritan woman at the well experiences the grace and omniscience of Jesus, and then she goes and tells the whole town about it (John 4)! Paul encounters the risen Christ on the Damascus Road and then becomes the greatest missionary to ever live (Acts 9). You don't get hit by a freight train and stay the same.

I am convinced: if our churches will be faithful to make the exaltation of Christ our goal, then Christ will be faithful to make His missionaries. The answer is not giving people more programs or things to do. Let's be honest: people don't want to "do missions" (or "do evangelism"). People are selfish, sinners who would rather be spokesmen for themselves, their businesses, or their favorite sports teams. "Out of the abundance of the heart, the mouth speaks" (Matt. 12:34). People naturally and generously give their time and their voice to the things they love. It's a deep-rooted, heart-change that is needed, and the only way that change happens is when the glory of Christ shines brighter than the glory of this world. It's when their heart finally *sees Jesus* and says, "WOW!" So the question moves from "How do we create missionaries?" to "How does God create missionaries?" God creates missionaries by putting Himself on display, so putting Him and His glory on display must be our aim.

Missions Exists Because Worship Does

There is no text that more clearly displays worship fueling mission like Isaiah 6:1–8. Read this well-known passage again, even if you have read it thousands of times:

> In the year that King Uzziah died, I saw
> the Lord, high and exalted, seated on a throne;
> and the train of his robe filled the temple.
>
> Above him were seraphim, each with six
> wings: With two wings they covered their faces,
> with two they covered their feet, and with two
> they were flying. And they were calling to one
> another:
>
> "Holy, holy, holy is the Lord Almighty; the
> whole earth is full of his glory."
>
> At the sound of their voices the doorposts
> and thresholds shook and the temple was filled
> with smoke.
>
> "Woe to me!" I cried. "I am ruined! For I
> am a man of unclean lips, and I live among a
> people of unclean lips, and my eyes have seen
> the King, the Lord Almighty."
>
> Then one of the seraphim flew to me with
> a live coal in his hand, which he had taken
> with tongs from the altar. With it he touched
> my mouth and said, "See, this has touched

your lips; your guilt is taken away and your sin
atoned for."
Then I heard the voice of the Lord saying,
"Whom shall I send? And who will go for us?"
And I said, "Here am I. Send me!"

In this well-known text, Isaiah sees God, sees his own
depravity, experiences God's mercy, and then responds in
surrender to God's mission. This is the journey of the missionary. This is the missionary's classroom. There are two
primary things in this text that are crucial to our understanding of worship and will help us in our aim to exalt the
glory of God above all things for the joy of the nations.

Put God on Display through His Word

The first thing to notice in this passage is that *Isaiah sees
God.* "In the year that King Uzziah died, I saw the Lord . . ."
Seeing God is where missions begins because seeing God
is where worship begins. Worship is a rhythm of revelation
and response. We see something magnificent (revelation) and
then we respond in adoration (response). So, in order to make
a people a worshipping people, we must help them see God.
But how do we do this today? It's the twenty-first century.
Jesus has come into the world and returned to the Father.

This is not the Old Testament, so God, as far as we know, is no longer revealing Himself visibly. So how do we see Him?

Many answer this question with things like: we see God in the sky . . . we see God in other people, etc. These answers have *some* truth to them (Ps. 19; Job 38–39), but these things (the creation) are insufficient revealers of God and will only lead to idolatry apart from the gospel (Rom. 1).

First, *how* do we see God? We see the Holy One with the eyes of the heart (Eph. 1:18). God is invisible (1 Tim. 1:17). He is Spirit (John 4:24). He says that no man can see Him and live (Exod. 33:20). God the Son has already resurrected. Thus, in our day and age, we must see Him with the eyes of the heart.

Second, *where* do we see God? We see God and His glory in the Bible. The Word of God is the revelation of Himself to mankind. Period. It's how we see God. It is Revelation. The Scriptures are the foundation of all Christian worship.

So what's the practical outworking of this? I tell worship leaders often, if we are not using Scripture in our worship sets then we are leading people into idolatry. If the Word is how we put God on display, which leads to worship and joy and mission, then we must be *filling* our worship gatherings with the Bible. We must preach it. We must sing it. Our songs must be filled with Scripture. Our praying must be filled with Scripture. Our benedictions and blessings must be filled with it. And the good news is: The Word of God does not return void! It is always powerful to reveal God's glory and change hearts. Always! If we as ministers are battling against the glory of this world with the glory of our own eloquence or talent, then we are waving a flashlight with a dying battery in an arena of LEDs and strobe lights. Open the Bible and you turn on the sun.

The way this works for me is this: when I'm leading worship and I have a moment I can share something, that something should be the Bible. I don't have time to tell people about my philosophy or opinions on this or that. I have two minutes to say something meaningful, so I'm going to quote Scripture. In those moments when I'm leading heartfelt worship and I look out into the congregation and everyone is looking at me like a herd of cattle, I open the Bible. Sometimes I even stop in the middle of a song to read from God's Word to remind people WHO we are worshipping. And you know what's funny? Ninety-nine percent of the time people begin responding. Why? They see God.

Put God on Display through the Gospel

The other place we see God is in the Story of the Bible. We see God and His glory in *the gospel*; the glorious news of the saving work of Jesus Christ.

Notice in this passage the crucial *order* in which Isaiah experiences God. He sees God, sees his sin, experiences mercy, and then cries, "Here am I. Send me!" What is this, other than the gospel? What is this, other than a summation of the book of Romans. We see God, the Creator of all things (Rom. 1). We see our idolatry (Rom. 1). We see the ruin of our sin and our utter separation from God (Rom. 3). We then taste and experience the fire of God's mercy, in that while we were yet sinners, Christ died for us (Rom. 5). There is no condemnation in such love, (Rom. 8), and in view of this mercy, we offer everything to God (Rom. 12:1)! The gospel is what reveals the glory of God's love and power. And the cross, at the center of the gospel, is, as John Piper said, "The blazing center of the Glory of God." What's the practical outworking of this? We must give people the Story! We must give them the cross.

Our churches and worship gatherings should be filled with the passionate celebration of the gospel. We must preach the gospel. We must sing the gospel. Our songs must be saturated with the gospel. One way this works itself out practically for me is in how I choose song sets. I no longer plan worship sets around doing fast songs first and slow songs last, or putting the songs in similar keys.

I just sing the Story.

I don't really ever begin worship services with "cross songs"—not because I think it's *wrong* to do that, but because the cross is not where God started His Story. God started His story with Himself and His glory. So typically I will begin with songs about the greatness of God. THEN and AFTER people have seen the greatness of God and their depravity, I will bring in the cross, because that is when it is infinitely important. Then I go to songs on the resurrection, surrender, and so forth. I tell the Story, because the Story, not my songs nor my voice, is the power of God (Rom. 1:16).

Missionaries are born in the incubators of gospel-centered churches. The gospel not only produces obedience to God and His mission, but the right *kind* of obedience. The kind that is fun. So give people the Story. For the sake of the nations. For the sake of God's glory. Put the beauty of God on display. People will fall in love with Him. People who are in love do crazy things, like change the world.

Worship as the Goal of Missions

But missions, as John Piper famously stated, also exists "because worship doesn't." Worship gives us the power to do missions, but it also gives us the purpose of missions. This is found all over the Bible, but is seen vividly in Revelation 5 and 7. In these passages, we see where history is heading.

We see the period at the end of the sentence. What is it? It is people from every tribe, tongue, and nation surrounding the throne of God, and worshipping the Lamb who was slain. That's the point of missions. And by "missions," lest we overlook certain people due to our favoritisms, we mean the taking of the gospel to all "peoples." Not simply "living missionally," although that is important. Missions is the taking of the gospel to every people group (Matt. 28:19). Jesus is *that* worthy.

The best way to illustrate this is through a story. John Leonard Dober and David Nitschman lived in Copenhagen, Denmark, in the early 1700s. They were followers of Jesus Christ, and in their early twenties John and David heard about an island in the West Indies where an atheist British slave owner had about three thousand slaves. None of them were allowed to ever hear the good news of the gospel. They heard no missionaries were allowed on the island, so the slaves were simply left to live and die without ever hearing of Christ.

These two young men, profoundly disturbed by the news, made the decision to go there to reach these slaves with the gospel. Their plan was to sell themselves into slavery so that they could be among the slaves. That's right. These men would sell themselves into slavery. They weren't heading out on a short-term mission trip. This wasn't a two-year commitment. These men left to go and live and suffer as slaves and they had no idea if they would ever come back. Their families and their church in large part were against their decision, and questioned the wisdom and motivation of the whole thing. And yet, John and David prepared to go.

After great opposition, the two young men finally arrived at the pier to board their ship. Their families and friends were there to say good-bye, all sure they would never see them again. The men boarded the ship and set out. And as the gap between the shore and the ship widened, the two men linked arms, and one of them raised his hand and shouted across the gap these final words . . . *"MAY THE LAMB THAT WAS SLAIN RECEIVE THE REWARD OF HIS SUFFERING!"*[3]

Not "pray for us." Not even "pray for the people we'll be serving." They wanted Jesus to get glory; that's the point. That's worship as the goal of missions.

Conclusion

My hope is, in these pages, you have seen the intricate relationship between worship and mission. My prayer is that worship leaders, pastors, and churches who aren't really doing much in the cause of missions will see these words as a loving rebuke. This is not a call to "do more" or "try harder," but a call to simply be faithful to put God on display in your congregation. Missions will follow. Ministry really isn't that complicated. We say, "Look at Him." They say, "Here am I, send me." The French writer Antoine de Saint-Exupéry summed it up well when he said, "If you want to build a ship, don't drum up people to collect wood and don't assign them tasks and work. Rather, teach them to long for the endless immensity of the sea." Give them the Endless Immensity. Give them God.

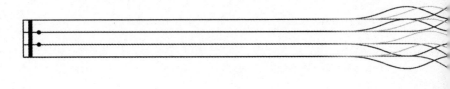

5

The Worship Leader and His Heart

Stephen Miller, Prestonwood Baptist Church (Plano, Texas)

On August 10, 1628, Captain Sofring Hansson took the helm of the Swedish warship, *Vasa*, and set sail for its maiden voyage. Thousands watched as the ship fired its cannons with all the pomp and circumstance befitting a ship in the royal navy. King Gustavus Adolphus himself had ordered its construction, giving specific building instructions and sparing no expense to beautify a vessel that would exhibit his wisdom, authority, and military prowess.

For more than two years, six of the most prestigious expert sculptors of the day labored intensively to craft elaborate, ornate sculptures with which to adorn the vessel. Few ships could touch the aesthetic appeal—it was truly breathtaking. As the ship set sail, a light breeze cooled the faces of the crew and spectators, when a sudden gust of wind filled the ship's sails, rocking it just enough to allow water to begin gushing in through its gun ports. Less than a nautical mile into its voyage, the *Vasa* sank. Fifty people died.[1]

The builders had labored extensively over the ship's external appeal, fueled by a hunger for the world's applause, but neglected to adequately attend to the ship's internal structural integrity. The *Vasa* was top-heavy and its ballast was not sufficiently suited to handle even the lightest winds, let alone a storm of any significant strength or magnitude.

I'm not a sailor and I don't know all the ins and outs of ships, but I do know there is nothing impressive about a ballast. No one stops to stare and admiringly exclaims, "My! My! What a lovely ballast!" It's not even visible most of the time. Its entire function is to sit below water where no one can see it, and steady the ship against the forces that threaten the visible, aesthetically pleasing portions of the ship. And yet without it, the ship sinks.

So it is with the heart of a worship leader.

Obviously when I say "the heart," I don't mean the eleven-ounce circulatory organ that sits in our chests and supplies blood to our bodies. The ancient Hebrew notion of "heart" means the center of all of our being. The source of all our thoughts, emotions, longings, passions, and desires—the core of our integrity and character. The character of our hearts, for better or worse, will necessarily shape everything we do in ministry. Like a ship's ballast, it will decide whether we sink or sail.

Worship pastors, like most pastors, stand on stage and proclaim the majesty of God for their congregation to see. They are public figures who symbolize private holiness and, therefore, are either drawn to their knees in regular, humble prayer, or are forced to become expert thespians, maintaining a consistent façade of righteousness.

Many worship pastors are chosen for their talents and successes, but have been battered out of intimacy with God by the pressure to continue to perform and succeed. Some are sinking and don't even realize it. Paralyzed by the fear of losing their ministry or respect, they cannot be vulnerable or transparent enough to admit they need time to invest in their own hearts and recover the intimacy with Jesus they once had. So they continue neglecting their own hearts, content to practice their righteousness before men.

But the ship is going down.

What Matters Most

> Beware of practicing your righteousness
> before other people in order to be seen by them,
> for then you will have no reward from your
> Father who is in heaven. (Matt. 6:1)

What's done in secret matters most. While the temporal dividends of regularly practicing our holiness in secret don't seem obvious, Jesus takes this entire chapter of the Bible to warn us of practicing our righteousness before men. He exhorts us to pray in secret, give in secret, fast in secret, and serve God faithfully, not for the treasures that we will receive here on earth, but for the secret, eternal inheritance that we have in Jesus Christ.

There's just one problem: Aren't worship leaders and pastors *supposed* to practice their righteousness before others? Aren't we supposed to be the light of the world letting our light shine before men so that they may see our good works and glorify our Father in heaven? Aren't we supposed to stand before people week after week and pray and teach, to be examples of generosity to the people we lead? Our people trust that because we are doing these things publicly, we must be spending time in secret before God, practicing righteousness throughout the week. This is a dangerous position to stand in because, so often, it is far from the truth.

With all the time and preparation worship leaders put into being excellent musicians, vocalists, band leaders, liturgists, and teachers, the single most important thing we can do is to stand before the Lord in secret. To go into a closet and listen to Him, speak with Him, adore Him, and confess to Him where no one else can see. We cannot marginalize private time in prayer and the reading of God's Word into handy tools from which to draw our latest song or sermon. We must *eagerly* pray and read God's Word in order to know Him better, worship Him rightly, and let Him change our hearts.

Worship in Secret

> Nothing is covered up that will not be revealed, or hidden that will not be known. Therefore whatever you have said in the dark shall be heard in the light, and what you have whispered in private rooms shall be proclaimed on the housetops. (Luke 12:2–3)

What we do with the time we spend in secret will one day be made known. In the same way that one can grow in intimacy with God in secret, the potential for sin to prevail can also be nurtured in private. R. C. Sproul sums up the above Scripture with this simple, yet grave reminder: "People fall in private long before they fall in public."

We know in the back of our minds that our secret will come out, but we believe it will be in the distant future, if on this side of eternity at all. We think we have ample time to entertain our private sin before it really catches up to us. In our prideful attempts to manage our own lives beyond and outside the will of God, we also delude ourselves into believing that we can manage the way our sin is revealed, or avoid it altogether. I'm sure that the captain of the *Vasa* knew that the ship would one day be put out of commission, but he never thought it would be so soon.

So many of us spend our time in the darkness, snacking on prideful thoughts of self-glory, thinking that such things are merely trifles, all the while acquiring such a taste for the counterfeit that we cannot remember the real thing. In our attempts at managing our image, we have become experts at putting on the mask of piety and practicing our righteousness to be seen by men, while our character and our personal, private holiness fade into the horizon of obscurity.

For many worship leaders, that means becoming consumed with building a bigger fan-base and better platform. More fans, more friends, more followers, more flattery—the secret thoughts of our hearts fuel our obsession with our own name. We lead people to ourselves rather than Jesus, and then wonder why power has left the pulpit and why the deep theological treasures of some of the old hymns have degenerated into songs that exalt us above the glory of our Creator.

Despite our pretensions, our pride grows more obvious each time we speak. We use the words *me, my,* and *mine* much more frequently, and the sweet aroma of heaven that once lingered on us turns into the stench of God's resistance. We ignorantly think we've fooled those around us, that we've gotten away with our attempts to replace God's glory with our own. Even if it were possible that no one sees who we are becoming, someone *always* sees. We are never truly alone, never truly hidden. As the psalmist puts it, "Where can I go to flee from you?" (Ps. 139:7). It's impossible to hide from an ever-present, all-knowing, all-seeing God, who not only sees what you do, but knows your very thoughts.

Everything done in secret will someday be made known—but only because it is already known. There is a perfectly just Judge who will one day call all of us to account for all we have done. All injustice in the world will be made right. While this is hopeful, it's a sobering truth to swallow when I remember all the things I have done, that I think I've kept secret: every little white lie, every lustful glance or thought, every envious wish, every prideful desire. None of it was truly secret and all of it will be brought to the light one day.

Coming Clean

> If we say we have no sin, we deceive our-
> selves, and the truth is not in us. If we confess
> our sins, he is faithful and just to forgive us our
> sins and to cleanse us from all unrighteousness.
> If we say we have not sinned, we make him a
> liar, and his word is not in us. (1 John 1:8–10)

When we sin, it's always better to voluntarily confess than to be forced to admit. As leaders and pastors, it is often hard for us to confess our sins to others. We take the scriptural mandate to be "above reproach" and confuse it with perfection, speculating that people expect leadership to be exempt from temptation. It can be exceedingly difficult to come clean about our struggles when we think that our reputation is on the line, or worse yet, our job. We take our sins, lock them away into a dark closet, put as many padlocks on the closet as we can, and cover the door with a Thomas Kinkade painting. We don't want anyone to see the dark secrets of our hearts.

I am just as much a work in progress as the people I'm leading. The Holy Spirit is teaching me patience and obedience and faithfulness. He is teaching me to love what He loves and hate what He hates, but this is a long, slow, and sometimes painful process. But it is hopeful, as Paul explains in 2 Corinthians 3:17–18:

> Now the Lord is the Spirit, and where the Spirit of the Lord is, there is freedom. And we all, with unveiled face, beholding the glory of the Lord, are being transformed into the same image from one degree of glory to another. For this comes from the Lord who is the Spirit.

Jesus is concerned with our hearts. He sees the long game. He sees each time we are derailed by temptation and He strengthens us to get back up and pursue Him again. Through all our faults and failures, He is graciously shaping our hearts, because He is overwhelmingly committed to making us like Him by transforming us into the image of His glory more and more each day. He has more than we could imagine invested into seeing this happen.

While much of God's shaping work of our hearts comes in secret fellowship with Him, it also comes as we live transparently in gospel community. God, in His infinite wisdom, has given us the church, our new redeemed family to help sanctify us. We should all strive to develop a community of grace in which we are overwhelmingly for each other, where we can confidently confess to one another and be met with love and truth, rather than condemnation and judgment. As we confess and repent in true community, we speak the truth of the gospel to one another, which God uses to shape us.

When I believe a lie, my community helps expose that lie and encourages me to believe the truth of who God is, what He has done, and who I am in light of that. Because I have been created in God's image, bought with His blood, adopted into His family, given an eternal inheritance, and indwelled with His Holy Spirit, I am set free from self-protection and trying to defend my reputation. I am free to be transparent and honest, to get out of the dark shadows of my sin and into the light of God's glorious presence.

His light gives us life. Just as plants and trees grow toward the light, so our hearts grow strong toward the light of Christ. The perilous detriment of sin is that it separates us from God, our source of life. Though we are justified and forgiven in Christ, sin still blocks the light of intimate fellowship with God. But as we walk in the light, confessing our sins to one another and to Him, He is faithful and just to forgive us our sins, cleanse us from all unrighteousness, and strengthen us with the light of His presence.

Worship leaders are always in danger of falling into the pharisaical trap of honoring God with our lips, but keeping our hearts far from Him. Our mandate is to *actually* love the Lord with all our heart, mind, soul, and strength—not to simply make people think we do. We are not called to be bright and shiny on the surface, yet deficient underneath. True saving faith will always be characterized by an inward heart delight in the person and ways of God, whether or not anyone is looking. It may take years or it may take an hour, but in the end, if we are not pursuing God and building our lives on Him, we will find ourselves with the *Vasa* at the bottom of the ocean.

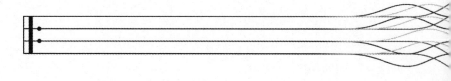

6

The Worship Leader
and Justice

*Aaron Ivey, Austin Stone Community
Church (Austin, Texas)*

A few years ago, I sensed the Holy Spirit prompting me to answer a convicting question: "Aaron, you're a pastor of people, intended to be an ambassador of justice and mercy. So how many relationships do you actually have with neglected, underprivileged, or impoverished people?" Internally, my response was something like, "Well, my church serves the poor, I support missions in Haiti, and I sponsor a few children through Compassion International, and so on." Don't get me wrong, these are all good things, but I couldn't shake the truth: I was not in proximity—in relationship—with the very people with whom Jesus spent His entire ministry.

This conviction prompted my wife and I to join a few other families from our church, The Austin Stone Community Church, who moved into one of the poorest neighborhoods in Austin, known as the St. John Community. St. John is only a few minutes from the lively and bustling parts of Austin, but this struggling neighborhood is scarred by a history of neglect, drug activity, prostitution, racism, and poverty. Only a few square miles of houses and schools contain some of the city's highest population of teen moms, fatherless children, and families caught in the vicious generational cycle of poverty. We purchased a home that had previously been used for drug activity and crime, and made it our aim to be a part of restoring not just a broken building, but a broken city, one relationship at a time.

We moved into our home in early 2010, and every day God continues to illuminate His heart for the poor. Being in the minority and usually separated by a language barrier, we have realized that serving the poor cannot be an agenda or project. It means living alongside the forgotten, and remembering their name. It means embracing a generation of fatherless kids by inviting them to jump on the trampoline in my backyard. It means having our lives disrupted by stories and tragedies, for with these disruptions comes a bruising and stealing of our hearts. From my children's perspectives, "the poor" is not an idea or concept that we'll one day need to sit down and teach them about. For them, "the poor" is their schoolmate. The "needy" is their best friend who they play soccer with. The "teen mom" is the young girl who waves every morning as she walks to Reagan High School. These are our neighbors. These are our friends. And it's given us a better understanding of the radical, loving, mercy-conscious person of Jesus who lived among people, walked their streets, and visited their houses.

What I'm saying is this: we cannot teach the idea of serving the poor and being people of justice unless we are altering our lives to actually live it out. I'm not saying you need to pack up and move to a poor neighborhood in your city; this is simply the direction God took my family. But the way you sacrifice and serve will always teach the people you lead better than any song could.

Gospel-Centered Justice

Jesus was constantly surrounded by the broken, the destructive, the bruised, and the unnoticed. His feet were dirty with the soil of the road. His hands felt the touch of the ignored and the weary. His heart moved for the unloved and lonely. His eyes emptied tears when sorrow and death seemed to stake its claim on a friend. Jesus was always in close proximity to pain and suffering, and to be like Him means we cannot isolate ourselves from experiencing the pain and suffering right in front of us. While the worship leader is typically isolated within the walls of a shiny church building, I beg you to settle for nothing less than steeping yourself, your family, and your ministry in the mission of Jesus to care for the broken. For, when you do this, you will naturally teach gospel-centric justice.

As artists, worship leaders, and pastors, we must have hearts that are willingly broken and stolen by experiences of poverty and injustice. It's only then that we have a truer sense of understanding and empathy for the world we've been entrusted to lead toward Jesus. This is what God did in creating us—He created us knowing that we would sin and rebel against Him. But in creating us, He was binding His heart up with ours and inviting us to a relationship. He knew we would wrong Him—rebel and sin against Him—though He demonstrates the depths of the riches of His grace and mercy through forgiveness. The contrast of His forgiveness with our depravity is a projection of the gospel.

We need to be willing to bind up our hearts with those who are broken by the effects of sin.

We cannot escape the fact that this world is more desperately broken than we are willing to admit. Our own cities and neighborhoods are full of despair, injustice, trafficking, and types of modern slavery. Though we train ourselves to ignore it, racial injustice, hate crimes, orphaned and abused children, and stories of extreme poverty pervade the streets of our shiny cities. It is the local church's role to seek justice and redemption of our cities, in Jesus' name.

Sadly, sometimes the world appears to be more responsive to the status of the world's brokenness than churches are. Our culture has embraced a crucial aspect of the gospel more than we have—restoring brokenness. Our culture is aware, informed, and yes, even broken over some of the world's greatest current tragedies. One could argue that there are more nonprofit organizations and a broader sense of awareness of today's injustice than ever before. Think about the number of clothing companies, local businesses, and advertisements for products that have embraced the idea of "giving back to the community" or devoting a portion of their proceeds to a specific cause, locally or globally. I recently saw an advertisement for a local bank that said, "Open a checking account with us and we'll donate $25 to the local food bank." The human heart is designed by God to have a sense of empathy and concern for what is unjust and broken.

Mainstream culture, which does not know Jesus, empathizes with pain and injustice. If we have been rescued, restored, and redeemed by a loving God, how much more should our hearts bend toward rescuing, restoring, and redeeming our neighborhoods and cities for the sake of His kingdom?

The church has not just been called to be aware, but to be a people who reflect the gospel of Jesus in the way we love, serve, give, and walk alongside the broken and neglected. You and I should not be merely imitating the culture's concern for justice; rather, we should be the example of what it looks like to reflect the gospel through justice. Social justice without the gospel is a counterfeit, merely a Band-Aid to a gunshot wound. Social justice can be sexy and glamorous, but being involved in seeking the redemption of the broken is messy, takes time, and rarely garners applause.

We, who have been infused with the good news of Jesus, are not just called to love and worship the person of Jesus, but to also love and seek the justice of the broken, as an act of our worship. Jesus gave two inseparable commands in Matthew 22:36–40: we must love God and people. Too many times, we worship with gratefulness for our own redemption, yet neglect being agents of God's redemption to our broken world. One of the truest postures of worship is to marry song and service, to live out the lyrics we sing through gospel-centered justice. Gospel-centered justice is a realization that since we have been loved, we then love. Since we have been adopted, we then adopt and care for the orphan (Eph. 1:5). Since we have been spared from physical and spiritual poverty, we also seek the rescue of those in physical and spiritual poverty.

After leading worship for nearly fifteen years, I have reached the humbling conclusion that a crucial role in the life of the worship leader is leading the charge in seeking justice, renewal, and redemption. I am tired of clothing companies and marketing firms seemingly leading the charge toward acts of mercy and justice. I am weary of governments needing to create programs to care for the very issues and needs that the church has neglected to concern herself with. The role of the worship leader is not merely to lead a congregation to sing well-crafted and theologically rich songs, but also to lead a people toward service as an act of worship. Beyond simply preaching "social justice," God has called the worship leader to consciously realize, reflect, and teach something much richer and truer: gospel-centered justice.

So, how do we become worship leaders who center our mission, songs, and leadership in this concept of gospel-centered justice?

Culture and Gospel

We must realize the redemption and mercy that we have been given. Yes, it might seem elementary, but I wonder how many of us actually have felt the gravity of the cross of Jesus, and what His death, burial, and resurrection means for us. We know the story and can even teach it well, but do we fully realize the implications of the gospel on our lives?

Culture suggests our ministry and our talent is a result of hard work and strategic networks, but the gospel reminds us that we were once dead and God alone breathed life into our lungs. Our best things, best talents, best creations could never impress a holy God, much less stir the heart of man toward worshipping Him. The gospel tells us that without Jesus, we would have no ministry, talent, or skill.

Culture tells us our merit and worth are found in the songs that we write, and the number of people in our congregation. But the gospel tells us that we have no merit or worth outside of God calling us His very own sons and daughters through Jesus.

Culture tells us we deserve happiness and success. But the gospel opens our eyes to the truth that we actually deserve hell, and the punishment we deserved was poured on Jesus instead. The gospel convinces us that happiness and success are fleeting and fragile, but joy comes with knowing and being known by Jesus.

Culture tells us we are enslaved to sin and held in bondage by its hold. But the gospel tells us that through Jesus, the chains of sin have been destroyed, exchanging our bondage to sin for a bondage to righteousness. Through the gospel, we experience true freedom in Christ.

As true worshippers, we must come to a place where we realize—literally, make real—the redemption and justice that we've been given through the gospel of Jesus Christ.

As those who realize the redemption and mercy we've been given, we must mirror redemption and mercy to those around us. No longer can worship pastors simply be satisfied with writing and arranging good songs, rehearsing them well, and asking people to sing them. We have a much higher calling on our lives—a calling to reflect the mission and way of Jesus.

Art has the uncanny ability to speak to the human heart in ways that others cannot; it has a way of translating the complexities of humanity and our need for God into ordinary language. Thomas Merton, an American author and Trappist monk, wrote extensively on the role of art in the church in his book, *No Man Is an Island.* I've been challenged and convicted at the seriousness with which he views artists. "The role of art," writes Merton, "is to stir the heart of man toward God—and anything that does not do that is not worthy of the label 'art.'"[1] Music, melody, lyrics, rhyme, and repetition all have a great purpose in stirring the heart of man toward God. As artists infused with the gospel, we have a unique obligation to mirror and reflect the heart of God through our art. Mirroring the redemption and mercy we've been shown by Christ should be one of the most natural things we do as artists; it should be as fluid and organic as inhaling fresh wind into our lungs.

Children easily understand the concept of mirroring. My four-year-old daughter, Story, has this down, although it usually gets her and me both in trouble. If I kick the dog, she kicks the dog. If I kiss her mom, she kisses her mom. If I belly-laugh at the dinner table, she belly-laughs. The point is simply this: children mimic their parents, both the good *and* the bad. And if our heavenly Father is the perfect example of mercy and redemption, then as His children we are created to mimic His mercy and redemption to those around us. Our worship shouldn't be restricted to songs, but must be expressed through serving, giving, and being merciful as we reflect the One we worship.

With this responsibility comes a great warning in our worshipping. Let's remember the harsh words in the Old Testament book of Amos.

> I hate, I despise your feasts, and I take no
> delight in your solemn assemblies. Even though
> you offer me your burnt offerings and grain

offerings, I will not accept them; and the peace
offerings of your fattened animals, I will not
look upon them. Take away from me the noise
of your songs; to the melody of your harps I
will not listen. (5:21–23)

At first glance this seems like something that goes against
the very nature of God, doesn't it? God always takes delight
in the songs of His people, right? Doesn't God love when His
people sing loud songs, take an offering, and then eat? But
there's something much deeper taking place in the book of
Amos that brings God's reaction of "hate" and "despise" to
this group of people who appeared to have all the postures of
worship that usually pleased God. The people of Israel had
great songs and offerings in this season, but their lives were
also laced with an abuse of the justice and righteousness they
had been given by God. Soaring melodies of choruses and
the scents of animal roasts filled the air, but in their wake
was neglect for the poor and disregard for the things that
pleased God most.

They gave justice only to those who could afford it (v. 10).
They trampled and took advantage of the under-resourced
and the poor (v. 11). They tainted the beautiful concept of
justice, making it sour and poisonous like the European
plant called "wormwood" (v. 7). They turned aside and gave
cold shoulders to the needy (v. 12); they forsook justice and

righteousness. Meanwhile, God grieved as they feasted and sang and seemingly worshipped Him. They celebrated God, but they stopped mirroring and reflecting Him to the people right outside their celebrations.

Richard Foster wrote, "As the cross is a sign of submission, so the towel is the sign of service." Bernard of Clairvaux once said, "Learn the lesson that, if you are to do the work of a prophet, what you need is not a sword, but a hoe." Too many of us want to be the prophet with the sword, but forget that being a prophet includes washing people's feet, feeding the hungry crowds, and asking some to exchange the throwing of stones for the giving of mercy. Being a prophet and a leader means regularly stepping out of the celebration to gently disrupt the dry soil, bringing to it the refreshing justice and hope of the gospel.

My fear is, in many ways, we could be guilty of the same sins as the Israelites in the book of Amos. As worship leaders, I pray we hear the plea and command of God, when He says, "But let justice roll down like waters, and righteousness like an ever-flowing stream" (Amos 5:24). Our sense of justice isn't meant to be sour and poisonous as wormwood, but rather a refreshing and ever-flowing stream of mercy, mirroring and reflecting God's heart for justice and mercy.

There's an old Puritan prayer that reflects a personal plea for myself, for my local church, and for you as you strive to mirror the gospel:

> Make me an almoner to give thy bounties to the
>   indigent,
> comfort to the mentally ill,
> restoration to the sin-diseased,
> hope to the despairing,
> joy to the sorrowing,
> love to the prodigals.
> Fill the garden of my soul with the wind of
>   love,
> That the scents of the Christian life may be
>   wafted to others;
> Then come and gather fruits to thy glory.
> So shall I fulfill the great end of my being—
> To glorify thee and be a blessing to men.[2]

As those who realize and are mirroring the redemption and mercy we've been given, we must also teach this redemption and mercy. Our role as worship leaders is to use our platform, songs, and influence to lead others toward being people of redemption and mercy. We cannot teach what we're not living, but the opposite is also true: we will naturally teach what we are living.

I would love to offer a simple solution, recounting the next five big justice causes you should sign up for as a worship leader. I could create a list of links to mission organizations online for you to send money to; I could try to inspire you to care deeply about something I care deeply about. But we all know that approach isn't effective, and it's definitely not something that would take root deep within your heart and spill into every area of your life and ministry.

The way of Jesus is to have a heart that beats for the kingdom of God, to seek it first and foremost, and to mirror His hope for redemption and restoration to the world. The biblical worship leader is one who realizes, mirrors, and teaches the beautiful story of God redeeming a broken people, for His glory.

American Airlines, Seat 16A

There I sat, on the verge of tears, in seat 16A on a packed American Airlines flight from Port-Au-Prince, Haiti, to Miami, Florida. Minutes prior, I had experienced the chaotic traffic through the nation's capital, the sorrow of saying good-bye to missionary friends, and the whirlwind and insanity of customs in the tiny pre-earthquake Haitian airport. This trip was exceptionally difficult for me. It was one of fifteen or so trips I would make to this country, and each one seemed to get progressively less hopeful.

I sat in my chair next to missionaries and nuns and teenagers with fluorescent mission trip shirts. They were buzzing with stories of hope and progress; I was broken by what seemed like a never-ending story of disappointment and tragedy. They left behind suitcases of supplies and toys; I left behind my two children, Amos and Story, who we had been trying to bring home through international adoption for almost two years. Some passengers were leaving Haiti with photo albums filled with children laughing, houses painted, and mountains climbed; I was leaving Haiti with the painful memory of my son, Amos, standing on the top floor of the Real Hope For Haiti rescue center, screaming, "Papa! Please don't leave me!" as rivers of dusty tears streamed down his weary Haitian cheeks.

In 2007, we started the international adoption process of two beautiful kids who were both abandoned at Real Hope For Haiti, a rescue center that cares for severely malnourished and abandoned children. Years of bureaucratic red tape and a corrupt government slowed down Haitian adoptions, and we found ourselves pleading with God to do what seemed impossible—to end this process and bring our kids home.

As I write this, Amos and Story have been home now since 2010. Amos came home just a few days after the tragic earthquake; God literally did the impossible when He moved heaven and earth to bring them both home. I'd love to tell the whole story, but it would take many more chapters to brag on God's providence, sovereignty, and faithfulness in their story. We praise God for their homecoming, the journey that gave us a glimpse into the reality of the world. He's called us to minister, and to a much deeper understanding of the gospel.

Jesus said, "Blessed are the pure in heart, for they shall see God. Blessed are the peacemakers, for they shall be called sons of God" (Matt. 5:8–9). Because you have been shown immeasurable peace, be a peacemaker, seeking the peace of your city. Because you have been rescued, be a rescuer, freeing those in slavery and despair. Because you have been fed and held, go feed and hold, in Jesus' name. Because you have been lavished with mercy and grace, be a person of mercy and grace, infusing worship with justice.

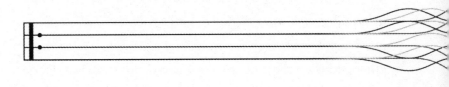

7

The Worship Leader and Liturgy

*Bruce Benedict, Hope College
(Holland, Michigan)*

For many of us, *liturgy* is a word that comes with a lot of baggage. Often, perhaps unfairly as we will see, it is associated with dead ritual and with worship that is devoid of the power and presence of the Holy Spirit. But every worship service is liturgical, whether we admit it or not.

Every worship experience, in its order and content, is an expression of the congregation's liturgy. It communicates something about your church, your doctrine, and the order of your priorities. Sometimes liturgy is casual and more informal; people are welcomed with a friendly word of greeting, a number of songs are sung, and a sermon is offered. At other churches, the order of worship is highly visible and feels more formal; there is a printed order of service with words to read and specific actions to follow.

I was a worship leader for a number of years before I came to the shocking realization that I was part of a team of leaders actively and consciously placing words in people's mouths (and hearts and minds), animating their bodies, and designing a gathering space for them to gather and become the people of God the Father, the Son, and Spirit. We were not just playing church, or rehearsing Christian spirituality; we were participating as characters in the greatest story ever unfolded in human history. We were the liturgical leaders responsible for expressing the heart of our congregation. And since that day, since the day I realized the gravity of my calling, I have never stopped being utterly terrified to lead God's people before His throne.

It is a high calling to be a worship leader. Through songs, prayers, and words, we help our church leaders proclaim the gospel, the full counsel of God's Word from Genesis to Revelation. Through our words and actions, we call people to stand in the glorious victory of the cross, to raise their hands in a united gesture of praise, to confess their sins with humble spirits, and bodies, to be sent out in mission filled with the confidence and assurance that the Holy Spirit is powerfully present and at work.

As worship leaders, we need to bear this burden with vigilant awareness. We have so much influence in this age. Our people ceaselessly strive to craft the sound tracks of their lives with songs that create an emotionally embodied experience of the world. We have been indoctrinated with a world of TV, movies, music, and concerts that have wired us to expect the stuff of music to lead the way:

- To tell us how to feel.
- To tell us who we are, and what we should love.
- To tell us whom (or Whom) we should worship.

In this chapter we will examine the *stuff* of worship and how we can wield it for the glory of God and His great gospel.

What Is Liturgy? The Stuff of Our Worship

In the past fifty years, the meaning of the word *liturgy* has come to encompass worship that thoughtfully engages and seeks to employ the full counsel of God and theology, through all the *stuff* of this world (people, space, technology), in order to present the most complete and compelling story of the gospel that we can. Bryan Chapell, in his book *Christ-Centered Worship*, says liturgy "conveys an understanding of the gospel. Whether one intends it or not, our worship patterns always communicate something." Chapell's book is an excellent resource for a brief overview of how liturgy has been used in church history.[1]

But an argument about the best way to do worship actually misses the point of the word *liturgy*. It is a word that has been carried throughout church history and is rooted in a New Testament word *leitourgia* (Rom. 12:1; Heb. 8:6), which can be broken down into two Greek words meaning "work" and "people," and is often translated as "the work of the people." Liturgy could be broadly defined as an act of service that was personal (a gift of a citizen), spiritual (work of the priests), or it can even have a militaristic context. Building off of Romans 12:1, we want our worship and our liturgy to encourage everyone to be actively involved and not merely be spectators. Even though the people may not sing every song or always look like they are engaged, our goal is to invite everyone to give of themselves in heart, mind, body, and soul.

Our liturgies strive to make us something as a group that we aren't as individuals. This is where we as Americans uniquely struggle because of our cultural individualism. Alexander Schmemann, a Russian Orthodox writer, has been helpful for many in the evangelical world on this topic. Schmemann reminds us that in worship we cease to become a collection of mere individuals, but through the work of worship we "become something corporate." We become the body of Christ—we become the bride of the King. This vision of the people of God as a spiritually unified group is what makes the gospel compelling!

So, in worship we must strive, above all, to serve one another and God. God serves us through the Spirit, the giver of gifts; we serve one another by the giving of gifts and the giving of ourselves; and in all this we are reminded that the Spirit is at work, uniting us together.

Liturgy as Good Storytelling

Now that we have the groundwork laid, we can precede to the good stuff: considering the story of Scripture and how it should inform our worship.

Worship leaders, you are storytellers. And no storyteller is any good if they don't know the story they're telling. Inside and out. Backward and forward.

Unfortunately, we too often get distracted by the *other stuff* of our services—sound systems, instruments, lighting, and video work—that lead us away from keeping the main thing the main thing.

Our calling, as worship leaders, is distinct from the preacher's. Paul Westermeyer says it well when he writes that we are "not called to know every theological detail, nor to unravel every theological question." What we do need is the ability "to step back and keep the whole story in perspective and to know its broad outlines and themes." This starts with having a basic grasp of the major redemptive acts in God's history.

Creation: God created the world and everything in it. His creation was perfect, holy, and good. Adam and Eve were created to live in peaceful relationship with God. They were to have dominion over the earth, to multiply and fill the earth, and to join in the eternal praises of the Triune God.

The Fall: Adam and Eve were deceived by the serpent into disobeying God's commands. Their disobedience in the garden gave birth to sin and shame, which marred creation and separated all of mankind from God. Adam and Eve were exiled from the garden. All of humanity, from Adam and Eve to those living this very day, is now separated from God and bound in sin and death.

Redemption: God continues to pursue His rebellious creatures, never ceasing to be faithful. He establishes a covenant with humanity, and promises that one day He will send a Son to rescue and redeem them. At the appointed time and place, God sent His only begotten Son, Jesus, into the world, so that whoever believes in Him should not perish but have eternal life. Jesus would suffer at the hands of the world and be crucified on the cross. Yet, after three days in the grave, He would rise again to new life and ascend back to the Father's throne, showering the children of God with the Spirit of God. The church, created by Christ's ordinance and through Jesus' union with sinners through the Holy Spirit, perseveres today for God's redemptive purposes.

Consummation: Jesus promised He would return to complete the consummation of the Father's redemptive plan, that is, the arrival of the kingdom of God. Through His redemption He will bring everything under the subjection of His power, authority, and rule. The book of Revelation is full of the images of consummation (both of covenant blessing and curse) and illustrates biblical worship. As worship leaders we must struggle to discern the teaching in this book—it is the end goal toward which we direct our people. Our prayer should be that our people desire to live with longing and hope for the future consummation of this kingdom.

Old Testament Worship— the First Worship Service

Now that we have taken some time to orient ourselves to the Bible's major story line, we can begin to examine how the Bible may suggest we structure our own worship services.

The first scene in Scripture that we would recognize as corporate worship takes place on the top of Mount Sinai in Exodus 24. This whole exchange is concerned with establishing a covenant between God and the people of Israel. "Covenant renewal" is one of many biblical undercurrents that are present in our worship. Here God speaks to Moses and commands that Moses, Aaron, and the elders of Israel shall come worship from afar. But only Moses alone shall "come near." This is the quintessential picture of God calling His people to worship.

After his descent from Sinai, Moses then shares "all the words of the Lord and all the rules" with the people. All the people respond to God with one voice and say, "All the words that the Lord has spoken we will do" (v. 3).

Here is the very heart of biblical worship: God speaks, and we respond. This fundamental principle of "revelation and response" should guide every form and part of our worship service. God speaks through His Word, through His Son, through His Holy Spirit, and we respond in covenant faithfulness through our words, our songs, our bodies, our service to each other, and, ultimately, to the world.

After Moses' meeting with God, he built an altar, offered burnt offerings, and sacrificed peace offerings to the Lord. Moses kept half of the blood and threw the rest against the altar. Here's our sacrifice and confession of our need for God's mercy. Here's the shadow of all that Jesus will accomplish one day as our Lamb of God. New Testament worship must, therefore, reflect the redemptive sacrifice foreshadowed in the Mosaic covenant and fulfilled through the new covenant. Our liturgy must reflect it as well; it will often be a time of contrition through song, prayer, or written confession.

After Moses finished reading the Word, the people responded again, "All that the LORD has spoken we will do, and we will be obedient" (v. 7).

In my church we always respond to the sermon with a song. This is a powerful place in the service because the Bible says that the Word always elicits a response, and I want to give my people a full-bodied way of expressing their love for God (Isa. 55:11). When I first began to study this passage, I was struck by how singing is a way of expressing obedience and renewing my covenant faithfulness to God!

After hearing the people's response, Moses took the remaining blood and threw it on the people and said, "Behold the blood of the covenant that the LORD has made with you in accordance with all these words" (v. 8). Doesn't this language sound eerily familiar? Doesn't it remind us of the words of Jesus during the Last Supper: "This cup that is poured out for you is the new covenant in my blood" (Luke 22:20)?

Then the Bible says that Moses and Aaron and the leaders of Israel went up to the top of Mount Sinai and (literally) "saw the God of Israel." God allowed them to sit in His presence, through the sacrifice of the covenant, and the Bible says, "They beheld God, and ate and drank" (Exod. 24:11).

Reading through this passage, I was shocked by how similar it was to the worship services I experienced in my life. Yet, I had never realized that it was a part of a biblical pattern of worship that God Himself established for His holiness and my access to His presence. We see the Word and table are central to the way that God leads us to Himself. We are called, we are sanctified, and we are brought into His presence to feast with Him.

But certainly we can't stop here.

New Testament Worship—
Jesus Changes Everything

We know that, with the coming of Jesus, everything changed. We know much of the worship and ritual of the Old Testament ceased because of the once-for-all sacrifice of Jesus as the Messiah of God. He came to be the perfect Lamb of God, to take away the sins of the world. So what does worship look like in the New Testament?

A great place to start is Acts 2. Jesus died, rose from the grave, and ascended to heaven to be exalted at the right hand of the Father. He sent the promised Holy Spirit, who clothed His new church with power so that they would continue His mission on earth and be His body on mission. Peter took up His mantle as the lead apostle and preached to everyone present, "Repent and be baptized." Later, this new group of believers gathered together and devoted themselves to the apostles' teaching and the fellowship, to the breaking of bread and prayer.

Here we have many of the same basic building blocks that we saw in Exodus 24. First, we see that they are gathered together to worship God after being initiated into the community through baptism. They attend to the hearing and teaching of God's Word (in this instance the words of the apostles), and they respond with acts of service and fellowship. They break bread together, celebrating the union they have with God, Jesus, and each other—remembering Jesus as He instructed them, celebrating what we know as the Lord's Supper. And they offered prayers of sacrifice and praise, including old psalms and new songs (1 Cor. 14:26).

While this passage in Acts is fundamental to appreciate the freedom of worship expression we have in Christ, it is only a beginning point and must be read in balance with the rest of the New Testament.

As the gospel spreads across the Mediterranean Sea, we see worship practices begin to thicken and mature. Paul addresses issues of worship in 1 Corinthians 8–14, and lists a host of admonitions for the young Timothy, as he plants churches and raises up leaders: "devote yourself to the *public* reading of Scripture, to exhortation, and to teaching"; and make "supplications, prayers, intercessions, and thanksgivings . . . for all people" (1 Tim. 4:13, emphasis added; 1 Tim. 2:1).

The book of Hebrews is a virtual pedagogy of worship, extolling Christ as the true and better high priest, superior to Moses and the law. Yet, even in the midst of this heavenly treatise, the author exhorts his readers, saying, "Let us consider how to stir up one another to love and good works, not neglecting to meet together, as is the habit of some, but encouraging one another, and all the more as you see the Day drawing near" (Heb. 10:24–25).

The book of Revelation concludes the New Testament with an encyclopedic range of worship expressions. In fact, one thing that the book of Revelation seems keen on communicating to us is that heavenly worship will encompass the best of the whole canon of Scripture—Revelation 15 presents us with a new arrangement of the old standard the "Song of Moses," now written with a new chorus of the "Song of the Lamb."

Biblical Elements of Liturgy

We can see from the brief overview below, harvested from the examples above, that the Bible offers a consistent pattern of worship. Below is a list of liturgical elements of worship that are embraced by the widest realm of the church. Each one of them can be accomplished in five to ten different ways, and you should experiment with ways you can communicate each element in your own context.

1. Call to Worship/Gathering Call: God summons us to the assembly to worship.

2. Purification/Confession: We confess our sins, and God cleanses us in Christ by forgiving our sins on the basis of Jesus' death as our substitute.

3. Consecration/Ascension/Praise: God enables us to "ascend" to heaven through the Spirit and have a special audience with the ascended Lord Jesus, where we lift up our hearts with joyful praise to join the worship of heaven around His heavenly throne (Eph. 2:6; Col. 3:1–3; Heb. 12:18–24; Rev. 1:4–5).

4. Word/Scripture/Teaching: Invited before God's throne, God speaks to us in the reading and preaching of His Word in Scripture, which transforms us and re-consecrates our lives by calling us afresh to embrace our new life and identity in Christ and to

113

live in a way that is consistent with that identity (Heb 4:12).

5. Offering/Thanksgiving: We respond to the ministry of the Word of God by offering ourselves to God in prayer; by confessing our renewed faith, love, and loyalty to God; and by giving material gifts of money and goods to serve the mission of Jesus' kingdom.

6. Communion/Lord's Supper/Eucharist: We eat at God's table, where God celebrates peace and friendship with us by serving us nothing less than Himself in the person of Jesus Christ. In this sacred meal, Jesus is both the host who presides and the food that we receive through bread and wine.

7. Blessing/Benediction: God sends us out into the world to serve Him with His blessing.[2]

Helps for Worship Planning

In the history of preaching, there is a practice referred to as *lectio continua,* or expository preaching, in which pastors preach through entire books of the Bible. Churches often employ expository preaching because it requires preaching both the easy and difficult passages of the Bible.

I think as worship leaders, we can also benefit from this type of thorough and consistent approach to worship leadership. For example, I often struggle with the Psalms. I know this wondrous book was the songbook of Jesus, but I'm often unsure how to use it in worship beyond my own private devotions. Jesus loved to sing the songs of the Bible (i.e., the Psalms), and I want to join Him in that practice (Matt. 26:30). I have found three tools incredibly helpful to make sure the worship I plan and lead communicates the full counsel of God, both the inspiring and not-so-inspiring bits.

The first help is systematic and biblical theology. Get a good systematic theology text such as Wayne Grudem's or Michael Horton's and read it. Then, break out your song and figure out what aspect of God's story you tell the least. As this book's title suggests, theology should always lead to doxology.

The second help is similar to the first. Familiarize yourself with the great creeds of church history. These are the blood-bought fruit of the church fighting for its own doctrinal purity. And while they will never be biblically exhaustive, they are a helpful benchmark to measure theological orthodoxy. The Nicene and Apostles' Creeds in particular remind us that our God and our worship should be deeply and profoundly Trinitarian. Some recent scholarship, evaluating the most popular songs in the CCLI database, has revealed that American evangelicals aren't as Trinitarian in song as we are in our confessions. This is a travesty! Our creeds and our songs shouldn't be at theological odds with one another. We need to view a richer picture of God the Father, Jesus the Son, and God the Holy Spirit illustrated in our hymnology and in our people's mouths, brains, and hearts!

The third thing that helps me is the church calendar. Sometimes, we American evangelicals suffer from our tendency toward spiritual myopia. We get so wrapped up in one topic, one debate, or even one particular glory of the gospel that we forget how we fit within the bigger picture of redemptive history. I have found the church calendar to be a wonderful source of wisdom in keeping me tethered to the big picture. Working through the life of Christ every year, as my church moves in and out of various books of the Bible, keeps my theology anchored to the rhythm of Jesus' life on earth. And even as we focus on proclaiming the resurrection each Sunday, we need to be reminded that there is no cross without incarnation (Advent and Christmas). There is no resurrection without the sufferings and trials of the Messiah (Lent and Holy Week). There is no church without the Holy Spirit (Pentecost). While the church calendar may be contentious in some contexts, acknowledging where we are in the year, even simplistically, helps us remember where we are in God's big story.

God has given us sixty-six books. Let's try to worship through as many of them as possible in song and prayer. I love the way Tim Keller puts it when he says, "The gospel is not the ABC's of the Christian life; it is the A through Z of the Christian life."[3]

Conclusion

Our worship must rest in the tension between freedom and form. Liturgical worship provides a vehicle for God's people to boldly pursue Scripture-rich, Spirit-filled worship. And if we don't fight to keep the big picture constantly before our people, then the work we pour into each Sunday will be lost in the pomp and show. Our lives are already so riddled with distractions. We need to bring to bear the deep wells of wisdom available to us in the church's history in order to keep both ourselves and our flocks on the narrow way. We have to build a sturdy framework for the gospel story to be strongly rooted in our hearts and minds.

Don't fall into the trap that singing about this or that piece of theology can't be worshipful! The church needs us to help preachers communicate the difficult theologies of Scripture. Lester Ruth says it best when he teaches us that "poetry often does a better job than prose at communicating the paradoxical theologies of Scripture in a way that both maintains the tensions of Scripture and leads us to devotion and praise."[4] What a challenge!

Every week when we gather together to worship as the body of Christ, we are practicing what it means to be followers of Jesus, and we are preparing to be citizens of a heavenly kingdom. Through every element of worship—speaking, listening, praying, serving—we are sharpened by the work of the Word, and increase our Spirit-filled effectiveness in the world. When we understand the biblical and gospel rhythms inherent in biblical worship, we can skillfully and spiritually inoculate ourselves against worldliness for the sake of our mission in the world.

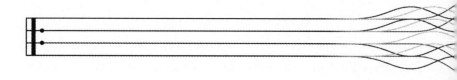

8

The Worship Leader and Creativity

Mike Cosper, Habor Media
(Louisville, Kentucky)

At breakfast once, my two-year-old, Maggie, began having an excited conversation with a sausage. When I asked her with whom she was talking, she held up the link and told me it was Olivia, the precocious pig who is the subject of her favorite books. While the irony of pretending that a sausage was a pig was lost on her, the joy of imagination was not. Her "Olivia" had an adventure around her plate, chatting with strawberries, playing in the oatmeal, and finally suffering a tragic end, eaten by a "Maggie-monster."

The whole episode reminded me that we are hopelessly imaginative creatures. It's an impulse that's been hardwired into humanity since creation, an echo of the way God made us. The Bible tells us that God took the dust of creation, shaped it, breathed life and meaning into it, and transformed it into something new and transcendent (Gen. 2:7). It's a foreshadow of our redemption, wherein God finds us once again in the dust of death, breathes new life into us, and transforms us again into something new and beautiful. Paul refers to this when he says we are God's *poema*, His workmanship (Eph. 2:10).

Creativity, then, is an echo of God's own creative work. We live in His world, taking what He's made, shaping it and making it into something new. Creation is raw material for imagination, transforming oils and canvases into portraits and landscapes, cotton and silk into wedding gowns and work clothes, and more complex amalgams into cars, skyscrapers, and iPhones.

It's as natural as breathing. All of life is shaped by our creative impulse, including worship. Whether we're talking about language, architecture, visual culture, or music, it all flows from the creative spark God has given us as image bearers.

When thinking about creativity and worship, it's not a question of *whether* we'll be creative, but *how* we'll be creative. Since creativity is a universal human attribute, your church is already full of creativity. Every church—from the most traditional to the most disastrously experimental—is making a host of creative decisions. The question to ask is, "How are we tapping into that creativity?"

Ephesians 2–4 paints a beautiful picture of the life of the church. Each member, uniquely gifted, brings what they have to the community and offers it as a way of building up and encouraging others in their gospel-transformed lives. Pastors of worship should be attentive to how the creative gifts of the church are being nurtured and cultivated, and how opportunities to express those gifts are being stewarded.

Authentic Creativity Is Grassroots

It's easy, in our commercialized society, to simply buy a whole worship culture off the shelf. Megachurches export their music, art, and video. A whole cottage industry of church resources thrives on selling everything associated with worship—from candles to banners to vestments and bow ties. Some churches, wary of such hollow contemporary commercialism, may nonetheless be guilty of simply buying into the culture of a previous generation.

The alternative is to look for opportunities to empower creatives in our own context. Let the body of Christ within our local congregations use their gifts to serve one another with the whole range of the arts in worship. We need a vision of grassroots *cultivation*. We need environments where permission is given for experimentation, learning, and trying new things.

It's a stark contrast to a commercial culture of church and worship, where leaders simply purchase such encouragement off the shelves and catalogs of Christian booksellers, and the body passively consumes, or where servants in music and arts ministries are told to emulate note for note something that came from another context. If we're honest, that kind of consumerism is easy. Rather than making disciples and carefully discerning a context, we can simply purchase and import from others. But if we want to empower Christ's church to use their gifts, to serve one another, to build each other up, and spur one another on in the midst of evil days and impending judgment, it's worth the effort.

To do this, we need to learn more about our church: What do they love? What do they listen to? How do they celebrate? In many ways, cultivating authentic creativity is an exercise in contextualization. We're truly contextualized when the culture of our church is shaped and formed from the roots of the community, rather than outsourcing it from someplace else.

Authentic Creativity Is about Discipleship

Developing a creative culture requires mature, servant-minded, gospel-loving creative people. Worship pastors and leaders should focus on good, old-fashioned discipleship, helping people identify their gifts and equipping them with the theological vision for using them to serve the church.

Part of this means developing the creative leaders you have, rather than pining for the leaders you don't have. We might wish we had Radiohead for a worship team, but God has given us The Oak Ridge Boys. Don't despise the gifts God has given you. Instead, pastorally focus on teaching these artists to use their gifts for the glory of God and the encouragement of the church.

Not all of our churches are going to have world-class dancers, painters, actors, sculptors, or musicians, but we all have creative people in our pews. It may take some imagination to figure out how their gifts can be made to serve, but it's worth the effort. It will almost certainly require breaking the musical mold of Christian radio.

I once served with a group of church musicians at a large church outside Louisville. Each week, the worship leader would drill the band through four or five CCM worship hits, almost all of which had a four-on-the-floor beat and four chords. Often, they were all in the sacred key of G. The band begrudgingly plowed through the painful monotony, week after week. What was tragic to me was the untapped skill in that group. Two of the players were studio assassins, men in their late forties who've been playing music their whole lives. Occasionally in rehearsal, the piano player—a real monster musician—would start into a Van Morrison or Billy Joel tune, and the bored band would roar to life, nailing grooves and playing intelligently with one another. The potential in that band was amazing . . . and untapped. Instead, they were corralled back into pseudo-U2 mediocrity every week.

No one complained, just as no one will likely complain in our churches when we force their hands creatively. People love to play music, even if it's music they don't love, but as pastors and worship leaders, we should learn to pay attention to what they do love. We should learn to prefer their preferences, because it just might give us a window into our congregations' preferences as well.

Authentic Creativity Is about Service

Outside the church, artists are taught to be shamelessly self-promoting. Indeed, it's nearly impossible to succeed vocationally as an artist without a certain amount of attention to self-promotion.

But inside the church, the arts are meant to be a servant of something greater. In worship, they serve the liturgy, helping to awaken imaginations and affections as the gospel is proclaimed in word, prayer, water, bread, and wine. While creativity is beneficial to the life of the church, it cannot become the object of our praise.

Creativity is a wonderful servant and a wretched master. When worship becomes centered on creativity, or when pastors and worship leaders begin to treat the gathered church as a concert or lecture hall, disaster ensues. Pushed to its limits, we end up with the more outlandish stunts in North American churches: Queen covers for "special music," tanks and movie sets on the church platform, 24-hour live-streamed bed-ins on the church roof—spectacle over substance.

Few have better articulated the need for servant-minded artistry than Michael Card, who likens the work of artists who serve the church to foot-washing.[1] Jesus' own act of foot-washing was an act of utter humility: the King of the universe taking a posture that was considered too low for even a slave. Artists can follow His lead, seeking to bless the church with their gifts while remaining a servant.

Here, too, we come back to the idea of preference. Loving someone well means loving what they love. I don't watch princess movies with my daughters because I love Disney princesses; I do it because I love what they love. Likewise, mature creativity learns to love what others love, serving others with our gifts, cultivating their gifts, and perpetually seeking to wash others' feet.

Authentic Creativity Requires Opportunity

If we want to cultivate a vibrant culture of creativity, we have to be willing to give opportunities for creatives to serve in meaningful and significant ways. This is perhaps one of the most important and most risky aspects of cultivating an environment where creativity can happen. Creative work is time and energy consuming, and inviting artists to use their gifts to decorate the dusty corners of an annex isn't going to result in enthusiastic participation. We must be willing to give them a place where their work is seen and heard.

Instead of hedging them, invite creatives into long-range planning. Let them see where the church is going with sermon series and church calendars, and ask them to dream up ways of serving. You don't have to mimic what's been done at other churches. You don't have to put painters in the front corners of your room. You don't have to start an art gallery. Instead, you should put five or six creative people in a room together, invite them to dream of how they might serve, and then . . . you just *listen*. Good pastoral leadership doesn't require you to originate all the ideas, but it does require you to shepherd them in helpful ways.

What a Creative Culture Looks Like

God has diversely gifted each of us, and calls us to come together as brothers and sisters, building up and encouraging one another with the profound hope of the gospel. Creatives have a role to play in that gathering and encouraging.

While the gospel is a transcultural message, the actual worship of the local church is inevitably enculturated in the language, music, and visual arts of a given time and place. Even as a congregation might be stretched to embrace aspects of those who differ from them, they nonetheless do so as people from a particular context. Their cultural diversity is itself a part of their own enculturation.

When pastors learn to empower creatives (as opposed to importing creativity), it allows the congregation to lead worship through word, symbol, music, visual art, and architecture that uniquely reflects our tribe—our unique, local, context. This is contextualizing in the best possible sense: the gospel has impacted our lives, and we respond with our own celebration and proclamation of that changeless gospel. This, of course, isn't to suggest that we don't participate in the works of the historical, global, or contemporary church. Rather, it's simply to suggest that along with our participation, we empower our creatives to make their own contributions.

When the culture of a given context is made to serve the liturgy (through the creative work of the local church), it says to both the church and the world, "The Kingdom of God is amongst us. Our tribe and tongue has joined the many around the throne, worshiping the Lamb who was slain."

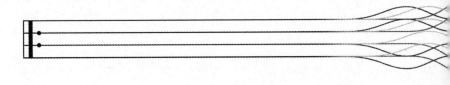

9

The Worship Leader and Disciple-Making

Aaron Keyes, Worship Leader

Several years ago, I began receiving phone calls and e-mails from various pastors I knew, who were looking to hire a new worship pastor. They wondered if I might know any guys who were available. The problem was that the guys I knew who were *available* weren't quite *recommendable*, and none of the guys I'd *recommend* were currently *available*.

Every pastor I spoke to was looking for a particular kind of worship pastor. They all had talented musicians who could lead a worship set; they had skilled vocalists who could lead the songs. They weren't looking for worship leaders who could lead *songs*. They were looking for worship leaders who could lead *people*.

Over a span of three days, I received three different phone calls from three different pastors. The first two calls ended with me saying, "I'm so sorry, I don't know of anyone right now, but I'll let you know if I think of someone." Sadly, I'd gotten pretty used to saying that to pastors looking for worship leaders. Finally, after the third call, I hung up the phone and wept. My heart melted for these churches; they were great churches that teach the Bible, love the Lord, and serve their cities. These weren't dead and dying churches hostile to the Holy Spirit; these churches were desperate and desiring to love God more deeply. They wanted to be led, but had no leader to lead. I became aware that the need for biblical worship leaders was far more severe than I might have imagined.

"Call me in a year. I'll have some guys for you," I promised after the last phone call. Something had to be done. I told my wife, Megan, about what happened and we began to pray about what we could do. I talked to my pastor, and we began to dream.

I began praying for God to use me to identify and empower the next generation's worship pastors. Up to this point, all I'd ever done to train worship leaders was offer some guys the chance to hang out weekly, go through some books together, and call it an internship. Now, God was stirring in me a desire to train and equip an army of worship leaders armed with God's Word and a servant's heart. When I began praying with Megan, we sensed the Lord calling us not simply to *internship* but to intentional *discipleship*.

The Start of School

In the span of a few months, God had answered some very specific prayers of ours and provided a house, a basement, and a bus to use to help disciple worship leaders. Now He just needed to provide the worship leaders. We spread the word about our new school, and had several guys apply to come live with us for six months. We laid the applications out on the floor and asked God to show us whom to accept, then set up interviews with each one. We ended up with two guys from Georgia, a Texan, and a hipster from Alberta, Canada.

In September of 2008, the students moved into a not-exactly-finished basement (you know how construction projects go), and slept on mattresses in our kids' playroom the first couple of weeks. We assembled IKEA furniture late into the night and ran around town picking up lightbulbs and plungers. We painted a whole lot of walls. I felt so bad for these guys. Here they were expecting to be in some great "class," and instead we were building and finishing their home for the next several months. It became very obvious a humble servant's heart wasn't optional.

We spent the next five months working through Bible study, theology of worship, and the spiritual disciplines; the guys wrote essays on different aspects of worship, leadership, and book reviews. My role was to critique their writing, and more important, disciple them as they grew in a deeper understanding of the worship of God. If I went to the hospital to pray with somebody, they tagged along. We tried to target all things pastoral and practical.

I'd give the guys a hypothetical worship service to build a worship set around, with a specific biblical text, a sermon idea, and a church context. Then, whatever songs or creative elements they'd come up with, they'd have to go back and find five to ten reasons or Scriptures to support each choice. Next, I set up a stool in the middle of the room and had them lead the rest of us through their set. They had to demonstrate how they would open the service, what they'd say or do, then do it. How would they transition between songs? How would they lead the congregation? I'd take notes, affirm what was good, and challenge where they needed to grow.

It was intimidating for the guys, but we were all *for* each other, so they were able to receive it. If they had a hard time speaking coherently while simultaneously playing, we'd work on that. If they had a hard time saying something that wasn't cliché, we'd work on that. If the guys weren't where they needed to be instrumentally or vocally, we put them in weekly lessons to help them improve.

At the end of that first year, we asked the guys to fill out a survey before leaving, and rate what was most impactful for them in their time with us. I was expecting any number of things. We had spent time with and learned from some of the most influential worship leaders in the world; surely they would write about how incredible it was to hear from them. Or maybe the spiritual disciplines like fasting and solitude. Maybe my brilliant Bible teaching.

Nope.

What every one of the guys described as being the most significant part of our new school was entirely shocking: *just being a part of our crazy family.*

Information or Imitation

Books, teaching, instruction, it's all important; but we fool ourselves if we think transferring information is the sum total of discipleship. Discipleship is more than working through curriculum, more than learning the intellectual content of the Bible. Discipleship involves us intentionally allowing the Word to work through us.

Jesus teaches us both how to be and how to build disciples. He models discipleship by doing nothing "on His own, but only what He sees the Father doing" (John 5:19 HCSB). Jesus said the very words He spoke were, "not my own; they belong to the Father who sent me" (John 14:24 NIV). As a disciple of Jesus, Paul became a disciple-maker as well, raising up leaders in the early church (e.g., Timothy, Titus, Silas, Luke, Epaphrus, Lydia). Paul would say to the Corinthians, "I urge you, then, be imitators of me" (1 Cor. 4:16). Later he'd say, "Imitate me as I also imitate Christ" (1 Cor. 11:1 HCSB). In every case, discipleship requires imitation, ultimately, of God the Father as seen in the life of Christ.

Paul's love for his disciples shines through in his letters to them. He writes to the Corinthian church as his "dear children" (1 Cor. 4:14 HCSB). I see the implications of Paul's call to his disciples to imitate him as he imitates Christ in the lives of my earthly children. I know they're picking up a lot more about life, love, and the Lord through the example I live out before them than the information I deliberately teach to them.

If we're merely teachers, and those under our care merely students, then our highest hopes for the next generation of worship leaders is that they learn some information. We'll merely need to *create curricula, develop resources,* and *set up classrooms.* But if we began to see ourselves as disciple-makers, then our definition of success changes drastically. We'll have to *create space in our schedules, living rooms, and hearts to allow our lives to intertwine.* To disciple like Paul, like Jesus, we'll have to step out of the classroom and into the world together. And it all begins in our home, and around the table.

In Acts 2, we read about the early church meeting regularly at the temple and in their homes (v. 46). They're in a regular rhythm of gathering corporately and gathering as smaller communities. I think a lot of churches have gotten very good at programming events, but I wonder how great we are at sharing meals. It's ironic that while I've spent the better part of the last fifteen years learning to lead in the corporate church gathering, investing in how I lead outside the home, our school for training worship leaders benefited most by what happened inside my home.

Discipling Worship Leaders

The days ahead could easily become a strategic window of opportunity if disciple-making becomes the most basic requirement in the job descriptions of worship leaders.

Imagine if worship pastors in their thirties, forties, and fifties began pouring their lives into younger worship leaders in their teens, twenties, and thirties.

Imagine the consequences if we skimp on actual discipleship, and balk on intentionally opening up our lives. If the only prerequisite to discipleship is to study a set curriculum, teach some practical skills, we may prematurely launch young musicians into positions where they are not prepared. If we mistake education for discipleship, this will be a watershed moment with bitter results. Jesus sent out disciples He knew, not crowds He taught.

Education is a vital part of discipleship, don't get me wrong. If we want worship leaders to "do as we do," they need to "know what we know." However, this is not all there is to discipleship. I've visited several Christian universities who have recently started "Worship Studies" degrees, and I've heard of churches launching new online worship training courses.[1] These are all fine things, but if our efforts are merely focused on information, they will fall short. They need to see you modeling your own walk with God, projecting a blueprint of godliness into the shadows of their hearts and minds. They need a disciple-maker.

By way of illustration, I have four sons; they all kind of look like me, talk like me, even act like me. They carry my DNA, but they're each unique. They don't look *exactly* like me; they don't act *exactly* like me. Ultimately, my dream for my sons isn't that they'd become *exactly* like me. It's that they'll become who God has uniquely made them to be, and that our time together will sharpen them in their own lives. I pray these things for the worship leaders I disciple as well. The blueprints we give our disciples aren't to produce carbon copies, but to serve as a reference for them to improve upon the design. Again, we want to train worship leaders who pursue greater things.

The Great Commission for Worship Leaders

Somewhere between overseeing Sunday services, songwriting, recording albums, and touring, we've let discipleship slip right through the cracks. What do our worship sets, services, albums, and songs even matter if they're not designed toward and rooted in discipleship? I only know a handful of worship leaders who are intentionally pouring their lives into the next generation. How can this be?

The Great Commission is just as applicable for worship leaders as it is for missionaries and pastors. It's very clear: make disciples wherever you go! It could be translated, *As you are going into all the world, make disciples* . . . It is far easier to write songs and record albums than it is to make disciples. We've got to do more than lead songs; we've got to disciple people. If nobody's following us Monday through Saturday, we're not leading worship; we're just leading songs.

These Days

During the twelve years of our marriage, Megan and I have never had as much fun doing ministry as right now, and one of the sweetest parts is doing it together. I'm often out leading or teaching worship, and Megan is often busy with her relationships and ministry leadership, but never have our individual gifts come together and complemented one another like they do when we're hosting, serving, and loving on the guys living with us. I'm learning that inviting young leaders into my home may be far more important than having them in my band or on stage.

Many worship leaders have come through our basement since those early days. I feel like we've learned more from them, and been more blessed as well. In particular, I'm learning to lead with *intention*, instead of just *intuition*. There is more intentionality to the structure of how we disciple guys, and I think it's getting better every time, but there is still much work to do.

For better or worse, worship leaders are shaping congregations. How many of our worship leaders would be recognized as leaders in their churches apart from their instruments?

Yes, worship leaders need to learn how to lead a band well, but more importantly, they need to learn how to become leaders in the church. Songwriters need to grow in their craft, but more importantly, they need to know how to grow in their understanding of Scripture. We need more than classrooms; we need discipleship of the kind we see in the lives of Jesus, Paul, and the early church.

A worship leader not only leads songs but leads people. My hope is to see a generation of godly and gifted young worship pastors arise who are qualified to disciple people in their churches. I'm praying for a movement of anointed and empowered worship leaders who would lead their churches *without* their musical contributions. I want to challenge you to open up your life beyond the perfect, polished, public projection and let people see who you really are. It may be difficult and leave you feeling uncomfortably vulnerable, but it will be fruitful. Sometimes it may be exhausting, but God promises a "crown of glory" for those who shepherd well and offer themselves as living examples for the flock (1 Pet. 5:2–4 HCSB).

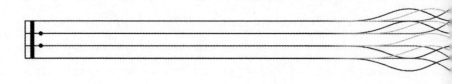

10

The Worship Leader and His Pastor

*Andi Rozier, Harvest Bible Chapel
(Rolling Meadows, Illinois)*

"You stick to the preaching, I'll lead the worship." Have you ever said that? If not, I'm confident you've probably thought it—or maybe I'm just the only one?

The relationship you share with your pastor is crucial to the survival of the role you serve in supporting him. That connection is as unique as a fingerprint. It's also a magnet for stress, pride, and conflict of agenda. These two roles, pastor and worship leader, functioning in unity (Ps. 133:1) and peace (Rom. 12:14) with one another during the peak of their church's weekly events will breathe life into the mission, vision, values, and even the creative functioning of the church. Discord between these integral roles is a huge target for the Enemy; harmony disarms him. In my experience, your relationship with your pastor will need persistent maintenance guided by wisdom.

My pastor, James MacDonald, is a passionate worshipper of Jesus Christ and frequently reminds our congregation that he preaches to make us all better worshippers. He explains how worship is not preparation for teaching, but the teaching of the Word promotes greater worship. He encourages fellow pastors and elders around him to realize God is so fired up about worship that nothing will substitute for them being the chief examples as worshippers in their churches. If they expect the worship leader to be the primary worshipper, there's a problem. James models leadership in worship authentically at our church. I've witnessed him shout to the Lord in adoration at the top of his voice with our congregation, and wept with him sitting at his piano as we have written a fresh song to the Lord. He is a man I deeply respect and love.

In the summer of 2001, I moved from a small town in England to Chicago. The United Kingdom (UK) is a country where it's almost impossible to get paid by the church to lead worship. I was now "living the dream" as an employed worship leader for a growing church in the north-west suburbs of Chicago. Until then, I had been part of a band that would lead worship around the country for small events. Whenever we interacted with a pastor, it was only for the short time we were at that church. Arriving in Chicago, it was clear from the start that James was hands-on with the content of our sung-worship time and in community with the worship team. Up until I joined this church staff, I had called most of the shots on what songs to sing. My ego was about to take a big hit.

One weekend, soon after being appointed to my new role, James instructed me to close the service with the hymn "Am I a Soldier of the Cross?" I had never heard of it. Up until that point—by chance—he had only picked closing songs I knew. Those were easy "directions" to take. This was new territory for me and I didn't like it at all.

With raised eyebrows, I first waited for him to second-guess himself, but I had to be on stage, so with teeth grinding I gave a compliant, "Umm, sure," as I turned and headed out the green room door. I took my place on stage to begin the service. My exterior said, "Good evening, church. Let's stand to worship the Lord," while my flesh burned with frustration that this guy would, out of nowhere, ask me to sing what I perceived to be some stale hymn. I assumed I would have had twenty-five better alternatives if I'd spoken up. My mind raced to extremes: *I'm the worship guy here, okay? You stick to the preaching and I'll pick the songs.*

[Pause film]

There it was. That was the moment for me when I chose not to be a team player—and also the moment I realized that to stay in that state of mind was not going to work out for me. The first time you thought something like that in frustration might have been over a completely different issue, but you get the point I'm making here. Being the worship leader doesn't mean you're in charge! So . . .

[Roll film]

Once the sung-worship time was over, I left the stage, pacing the backstage area, still acting like everything was okay. I eventually marched my way over to a small room that had a piano. After some intensive searching, our piano player found an old hymnal with the lyrics and melody to the song, and for the next thirty-five minutes, I pouted through retaining its seemingly obscure melody. It is shameful now, thinking back on it.

When the time came to return to the service, the two of us headed out on stage as James was wrapping up his message. I'd heard nothing of his message content up to that point, and as I continued to quietly hum the melody through in my head, he led our church in a prayer as he often does that sets the song up in a flawless transition.

I opened my mouth and began to sing . . .

> *Am I a soldier of the cross,*
> *A follower of the lamb,*
> *And shall I fear to own His cause,*
> *Or blush to speak His name?*

In a sea of faces before me, I began to immediately see . . . tears. Then, hearts exploding with conviction and voices lifting louder a cry to fight the good fight. Then more sincere tears:

> *. . . sure I must fight, if I would reign;*
> *increase my courage, Lord.*
> *I'll bear the toil, endure the pain,*
> *supported by Your Word.*

My whole understanding of the roles between pastor and worship leader came crashing down that day. I had put my pride before the task at hand, and the only person in that full room of worshippers whose holy fire remained unlit by the power of the Spirit's call was me. I had poked my "ministry eyes" out over a song, blinding me of the God-given partnership that my pastor and I have as we share the stage together every weekend. Understanding my role requires almost as much of understanding my pastor's role too. Our partnership is certainly more than simply agreeing on songs.

Who's Leading Worship?

When the pastoring of God's people goes beyond the stage for both of your roles, the worship leader's responsibility is still often centralized around his unique ministry, those moments of the weekend service when people gather to sing to the Lord. However, the pastor's role bleeds into the entire fabric of the church functioning properly. It's convicting to me that it takes my pastor a minimum of nine hours of intensive research and preparation for forty-five minutes of preaching. By contrast, it takes me, in honesty, a small fraction of that time in planning and rehearsing the sung-worship of which the message has often been pre-written by the likes of Chris Tomlin or Matt Redman.

The Sunday service is the main event in the church's weekly schedule, but the pastor is on call all week. His function in the church encompasses so much more than weekly preaching, and the sung-worship is not excluded from that role. God gave the pastor the responsibility of casting the vision of worship for your entire church. He is not just your *senior pastor*, but he is your worship pastor too. And it's crucial that you support him in that role and keep his vision in mind as you plan.

Submitting to Your Pastor

Hebrews 13:17 instructs us, "Obey your leaders and submit to them, for they are keeping watch over your souls, as those who will have to give an account. Let them do this with joy and not with groaning, for that would be of no advantage to you."

This is a poignant verse for worship leaders, and there's a lot packed into it. It calls us to obey and submit. As much as you desire for the people who are in your ministry to see and follow your leadership, it's so important that, in your volunteers' eyes, the same submission to leadership is duplicated as they observe your role under your (worship) pastor. Strength and health flow where that respect for authority is evident. And in your pastor's eyes, worship leaders who fulfill the joyful service Hebrews describes are submissive, humble, and recruiters for the mission of the church, placing content over musical preference. Worship leaders who understand their role alongside the pastor is a privilege, not an entitlement, are extremely valuable to the congregation. A worship leader who wisely serves his pastor will be in the best place to discover how God has used him to minister to his pastor.

Your congregation can pick up on both division and unity. They may not know what's wrong, or why it's wrong, but they will sense something is not right. Don't be fooled into thinking disharmony has no impact or has gone unnoticed. People in your congregation see it in their lives every day—with family, at work, and with friends—and if it's on stage, they will notice it too.

In maintaining and building this relationship, I plead with you not to fall into the trap that the primary place to develop harmony with your pastor is in front of your congregation on Sunday. Far from it! It's nurtured by intentionally finding time away from your instrument and the microphone, away from the pulpit, and away from the stage. That relationship grows as you seek out or even fight for a regular time and place where you can establish a mutual understanding not built on the content of your services or their success, but on the content of personal day-to-day life.

This person you're reaching out to is not an alien, even if you are laboring in the context of a generation gap. It's unique and sometimes scary to seek out a relationship with a brother who may be much older than you. The same rules of regular relationship-building apply: effort, consistency, patience, interest, and so on. I may not be on the top of my pastor's list to invite on vacation, but as I look back over ten years of relationship, it's filled with consistent fulfilled invitations from him to hang out and be in fellowship together, learning about each other's heart for the Lord, visions for the church, values for the ministry, our families, and music preferences. All of this lays a foundation for us to build an authentic relationship that won't falter in petty incidents. Maintaining it prepares the ground for leading God's people in what we call earth-shaking, window-rattling, and life-altering worship!

Relationship also doesn't come easy when your pastor is a very different personality type than you. The differences between a rationally driven, type A personality, and an emotionally driven, creative personality can be either explosive or complementary (the two accomplishing more together than they possibly ever could apart). In my marriage, I've often told my wife we're getting our PhD in knowing one another. We're two very different personalities, and the faster I get to know the way she thinks and behaves, the more we can achieve as we partner together. It's no different with this crucial relationship.

Our church has provided us the opportunity to take personality profile tests, which I recommend if you can afford it. There are a number of different options out there to choose from. The results are often hard to swallow because they hit close to home, revealing the real us, not our carefully constructed images. But the results are also encouraging, helping us understand the differences between our personalities and how our strengths and weaknesses complement each other.

Receiving Criticism

Hebrews 13:17 also instructs us to do our job "with joy and not with groaning, for that would be of no advantage to you." There's a joy rooted in the relationship you have with the ones who serve in authority over you. For example, consider how you respond to criticism. You labor each week over chord charts, band rehearsals, and sound checks. On Sunday, you and the band fire on all cylinders, leaving you with a good feeling in your gut about how the day went. But then, perhaps overhearing an innocent comment in the lobby, a church member wrecks your whole week with a mean-spirited attack on a song choice.

Didn't they notice the incredibly executed key-change in the third chorus? Couldn't they be a little more charitable, considering all of your strengths so clearly displayed this morning?

I've seen worship leaders abuse the relationship with their pastor in the same way. They often rush to harvest the benefits of their pastor's strengths, and are quick to fire a flare whenever they see a weakness. The writer of Hebrews doesn't have all of your preferences for leadership in mind when he exhorts you to work with joy, not groaning. Loved ones, this is not a relationship you should groan about. If you do, it will be of "no advantage to you." God has called you to something higher.

Another venue where conflicts arise, is when worship leaders seek honest feedback or are being invited to hear it. I love getting feedback, but often brace myself for more than just the content of the critique. Often, your relationship with your pastor is a complex cross section of relationships. Say, for example: when you've watched the game together on Monday, or laughed around the office (friend), and then had a great spiritual conversation on Friday (pastor), but now you're receive some critique on Sunday (boss); it's often hard to switch gears. The worship leader's reaction can easily become defensive and emotions flare. Who exactly is giving you the feedback? You'll be tempted to receive negative feedback as from a friend, like a personal attack, if it validates your emotional condition.

Your pastor, in the best-case scenario, has his mind on the mission of the worship service. So be ready to dial the emotions down in that moment and serve your pastor by being open to receiving the instruction—and acting upon it. It's a relief to him when he speaks into your ministry and discovers you share the burden of his mission. Be careful not to immediately take personal offense or assume your job or friendship is on the line, and don't forget, you're on the same team.

Go out of your way to communicate your willingness to share responsibility for the service. The more you do, the less your pastor feels like he has to carry the burden of worship service logistics on top of shepherding the church. After a time when I have received critique (yes, it continues to happen!), and I've had time to process appropriately, I'll often drop my pastor a text or an e-mail after the weekend service has finished. It's important he knows I'm on his side, but I'll also be sure to mention what I'm thankful for about him too (1 Thess. 5:11). Seek out and celebrate the strengths and giftedness of your pastor. I challenge you to write him a note this week and list three specific reasons you're thankful for him, and why.

In closing, remember this: before someone became your pastor and you their worship leader, you were both worshippers. You both still are! God is seeking good church leaders, but nothing comes close to His pursuit of worshippers who worship in spirit and truth (John 4:24). If you haven't already studied this passage in John, give it your full attention and make it the foundation of your roles as you serve together.

My prayer for you, reader, is this: that you would love God more than the role you've been given, and love the people of God more than the music you create. Now, go be a worship leader.

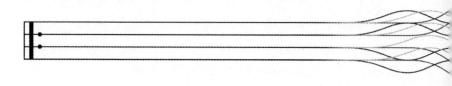

11

The Worship Leader
and Family Worship

*Matt Boswell, Providence Church
(Frisco, Texas)*

We were alone for the first time. My parents backed
out of our driveway and drove down our street, leaving my
wife, Jamie, and I crying together holding a brand-new baby.
They had been staying with us for the first week while we
adjusted to life with our newborn son, Caden. This was
our first child, and we realized we were now on our own.
In those precious days, I felt the gravity of being entrusted

with this fragile life in a profound way. God had called me to spiritually lead, protect, and provide for a family. He had positioned me as the shepherd of my family, and called me to disciple them in a home that worshipped God. He had placed me as the worship leader of a home.

As worship leaders, our primary task is to lead the people of God in the worship of God. However, for many of us, it is far easier to lead the people in our churches than in our homes. Some of us stand week after week leading our congregations in carefully thought-out song structures, articulate prayers, and strong leadership, but fail to lead worship within our homes. The great American Puritan Jonathan Edwards once said, "Every Christian family ought to be as it were a little church, consecrated to Christ, and wholly influenced and governed by his rules."[1] We care tremendously about our churches worshipping in a biblically informed, theologically rich manner. We should be equally concerned about the worship in our homes. With this in mind: How is your little church?

Toward a Theology of Family Worship

The Westminster Shorter Catechism begins with a booming question, "What is the chief end of man?" The answer reads, "The chief end of man is to glorify God and enjoy him forever." In this definition, we find a robust definition of what it means to worship God: glorifying and enjoying Him. It is not a stretch to extend this understanding to apply to the homes of Christians as well. The chief end of the family is to glorify God and enjoy Him forever. God is worthy of the worship of our homes.

Remember Who You Are

The stage is set. Moses is standing on the edge of the Promised Land, looking into what will soon be the homeland of the people of God. The journey has been long and costly, and the toll has been taxing on the people. Moses knows his life is nearing its end, and his words must penetrate into the hearts of his followers. He shapes their understanding of both God and their identity as the people of God. Moses carefully makes his appeal, aiming at the worship of God, the hearts of his people, and the homes in which they live:

> Hear, O Israel: The LORD our God, the
> LORD is one. (Deut. 6:4)

The Hebrew word that identifies this portion of Scripture is *Shema,* which in Hebrew means "hear," the first word of verse 4. From the beginning of the address, Moses is calling for and demanding the people's full attention. He is calling them to worship. He points them to consider first and foremost the character and nature of God. "The Lord our God, the Lord is one," he says, reminding them of the eternal, sovereign God who alone is worthy of their worship. In contrasting the God of the Hebrews with the pagan gods that would continue to surround the people, it was significant that the people have an accurate and high view of who God was.

Moses reminds the people whose they are, and who they are in light of that reality. As a boy, when I was around my Grandpa Easley, he would say to me, "Remember who you are and whom you represent." He said this first to remind me I was his grandson, and second, I was representing his name wherever I would go. We see here that God is "marinating" His people in their identity as the people of God so that as they walk in light of this reality, God will be glorified among the nations. In essence, Moses is saying to the people, "Remember who you are and whom you represent."

Worship in the Heart

Love the Lord your God with all your heart
and with all your soul and with all your strength.
These commandments that I give you today are
to be upon your hearts. (Deut. 6:5–6 niv)

Moses paints a vivid picture of what a holistic approach to worshipping Yahweh will look like. This command, noted by Jesus as the Great Commandment (Matt. 22:37–38), calls for God to be worshipped with all our heart, soul, and might. God commands the worship of the entire person, from the inside out. God desires to be the blazing center of the lives of His people.

We are often familiar with this part of Deuteronomy 6, though we fail to live according to its call and implications. Yes, we are the people of God. Yes, God has commanded we worship Him with all our heart, soul, and strength. But what will worshipping people look like from day to day in the outworking of our homes?

Worship in the Home

> Impress them upon your children. Talk about them when you sit at home and when you walk along the road, when you lie down and when you get up. Tie them as symbols on your hands and bind them on your foreheads. Write them on the doorframes of your houses and on your gates. (Deut. 6:7–9 NIV)

God first asks for the entirety of us individually, and then for the entirety of our homes. Notice how verses 7–9 highlight the centrality of life in the home, as God commands His followers to worship through the entire rhythm of life. The text here focuses specifically on the home as the continuation of our worship: "Impress them upon your children" (v. 7). The word *impress* here is an ancient ironworking term that means "to pierce repeatedly." The indisputable commission of the family is to be a transmitter of faith. The home should be an environment of spiritual growth. As Joel Beeke exhorts us, "The activities this text commands are *daily* activities that accompany lying down at night, rising up in the morning, sitting in the house, and walking by the way."[2] The intent of the passage is that God is glorified and worshipped in the homes of His people.

From the beginning, God's desire was for His name to be feared through the flourishing of the families making up His covenant people.

> Give ear, O my people, to my teaching;
> incline your ears to the words of my mouth!
> I will open my mouth in a parable;
> I will utter dark sayings from of old,
> things that we have heard and known,
> that our fathers have told us.
> We will not hide them from their children,
> but tell to the coming generation
> the glorious deeds of the Lord, and his might,
> and the wonders that he has done. (Ps. 78:1–4)

The Practice of Family Worship

The gospel takes ordinary houses and turns them into little churches. Our task is to lead our home and call our church to the reality and the sufficiency of the gospel. Revisiting the Deuteronomy narrative, Moses stood before the people of God and ascribed greatness to Him. He reinforced to the children of God their identity as a chosen people. He called them to worship in response to the God of their salvation.

In our home, my goal is the same. I want my wife and children to be reminded daily of the character and nature of God, and the glories of the gospel. I want them to be reminded of their identity and acceptance by God, not based on their performance, but because of His will. I also want to call them to live lives of worship.

In our home we practice this as we walk along the road and when we sit at home. While we want to make the most of every opportunity throughout the day, we also have special times every day we have set aside to worship together. While this isn't a *rigid* time and place, it is a *regular* time and place.

Build Your House on the Word of God

Many worship leaders stand in front of their congregations and profess the primacy of Scripture, but then enter their homes and fail to connect these truths to our lives. We boldly profess that the Scripture is inerrant and sufficient, but often fail to emphasize its authority and practice in our homes. If we want our families to be equipped for gospel living and empowered for gospel ministry, we must be a people who rely on the sufficiency of Scripture.

> All Scripture is breathed out by God and profitable for teaching, for reproof, for correction, and for training in righteousness, that the man of God may be competent, equipped for every good work. (2 Tim. 3:16)

Scripture is profitable for teaching our families. It corrects and shapes us. It trains us, so that our homes will be places where God is worshipped, and worshipped rightly.

Ways to Use Scripture in Family Worship

During family worship time, we read the Scriptures together as a matter of first importance. I want to model for our children what it looks like for their dad to love the Bible. My goal is to develop in them a lasting love for Scripture. I want them to see that what their dad says at church, he lives out at home. When we had four children under seven years old, we usually read from a children's storybook Bible, a psalm or proverb, or a very short narrative passage. During our reading there were (many) questions (often unrelated to the Scripture), and squirming, and arguing, and craziness. It was wild, and we loved it. Then and now, we don't over-formalize our time in Scripture. We adapt to where our children are at, meet them there, and trust God for the results.

One of the values we have is teaching our kids that Jesus is the focus of the entire biblical narrative.[3] In reading the account of Abraham being tested by God with the sacrifice of Isaac, one of our daughters asked why God would ever kill an innocent ram. Jamie and I laughed to each other, and were humored by her observation. We talked about it, and laughed a lot, and had the chance to point our kids to Christ.

Regardless of the ages and dynamics of your family, you can do three things to make time in Scripture engaging for your kids:

1. Contextualize for your family.
2. Be intentional with your time.
3. Have fun! Involve everyone, take turns reading, act out Scripture.

Read the Bible with Your Spouse

Having a regular time in the Scriptures with my wife is a very high value. We began this practice when we were engaged, and have done it almost daily for over twelve years now. For many of us, the thought of reading Scripture with our spouse has never crossed our mind. I want to encourage you to try it for a week, and see what God will do in your marriage as you open up the living Word of God together. We typically read through a book of the Bible or some devotional material, and the time is usually brief.

The goal is not to get through the Scriptures, but to get the Scriptures through us. Be encouraged by these words from Thomas Watson: "The reason we come away so cold from reading the Word is, because we do not warm ourselves at the fire of meditation."[4] My goal is that every night before Jamie falls asleep, the last thing she hears is her husband reading the Scriptures to her and praying for her. I want to leave this kind of legacy for my sons and daughters. I don't intend to create a new law for myself or my family, but to demonstrate what it means to live as a practicing worshipper.

Read Scripture personally, with your spouse, and with your kids.

Shape Your Home into a House of Prayer

When I counsel marriages, I usually ask how often the couple reads the Bible together, and how often they pray for one another. I have found very few families feel equipped to pray with one another outside of meals and special occasions. A pastor's wife even told me once that her husband had never led her in prayer during fifteen years of marriage. Charles Spurgeon said of praying together in the home:

> I trust there are none here present, who profess to be followers of Christ who do not also practice prayer in their families. We may have no positive commandment for it, but we believe that it is so much in accord with the genius and spirit of the gospel, and that it is so commended by the example of the saints, that the neglect thereof is a strange inconsistency.[5]

Having our family pray together is one of our most enjoyable experiences. We pray together as we "come and go" throughout the day, and at specific times of the day.

Pray as a Family

When we pray as a family, it is not an hour-long silent intercession for the 10/40 Window every time. With toddlers and small children, our prayer life is very raw and very entertaining. Most nights during bedtime prayers, our six-year-old would pray for "Goldie, Fishsticks, Tow Mater, Rainbows"—all fish. Some were dead fish, which I accidentally killed while changing their tank. He smiled as he said their names, knowing they are dead, and I smiled because I knew he forgave me, though it still was a shaping experience for him. I smiled, above all, because I knew his prayers were genuine and he was truly thankful.

Prayer as a family doesn't have to be a formal, liturgical time. We pray with our children about things happening in their lives. We pray for our neighbors and friends who need the gospel. We pray for the child we support through Compassion International. We pray and encourage our kids to pray. When they were smaller, we shaped their prayers by praying a sentence and having them repeat it. As they grow, they are able to pray on their own. The things they pray for and thank God for often amaze us. Because we want to teach our children the gospel is the most precious thing to us, we end all of our family prayers with, "Thank You for the gospel." We hope this will create a lasting memory of gratitude and dependence on Christ (Ps. 78:4). Each family will do this differently, but this is what works for us.

1. Don't pray too long.
2. Pray about things that occur in daily life (family, friends, neighbors, your church, etc.).
3. Manage your expectations on the richness of family prayer. A culture of prayer develops over time.

Pray with Your Spouse

With the prevalence of divorce in the church, even in ministry homes, cultivating prayer in a marriage is a necessity. There is built-in accountability that comes with praying together as a couple. One of my favorite things in the world is to hear my wife pray for me. I want to know that she is praying for me while I am at work, and what kinds of things she is asking the Lord to do in my life. I want her to know how I am leading her by praying for her. I want her to know she is being lifted before the Lord in the petitions of her husband. In this environment of prayer, is an intimacy that enriches and sustains the covenant of marriage. This is exactly what is in Peter's mind as he writes:

> You husbands in the same way, live with
> your wives in an understanding way, as with
> someone weaker, since she is a woman; and
> show her honor as a fellow heir of the grace of
> life, so that your prayers will not be hindered.
> (1 Pet. 3:7)

Repentance should be a common practice in Christian homes. As I write this, Jamie and I have both had to repent to our children for ways we handled situations today. Repentance is a sign of health in a home. When we repent of sin, we are showing our spouse and our children that we are sinners and in need of a great Savior.

Let Worship Be the Soundtrack of Your Home

Christians are a singing people. Singing has marked our faith from Exodus 15 with the Song of Moses, and continues through Revelation 5 as we sing the Song of the Lamb. We are a people with a song to sing (Pss. 96; 105:1–5). John Newton, the author of "Amazing Grace," writes about family worship:

> I think . . . that reading a portion of the Word of God should be ordinarily a part of our family worship; so likewise to sing a hymn or psalm, or part of one, at discretion; provided there are some people in the family who have enough of a musical ear and voice to conduct the singing in a tolerable manner: otherwise, perhaps, it may be better omitted.[6]

Take advice from one of the most prolific songwriters in church history: Singing is an important part of the Christian home.

Exhorting worship leaders to sing in their home feels like exhorting fish to swim. However, I know we are tempted to segment our lives between worshipping at church and worshipping in our "little church." Singing as a family does not have to be ritualistic or routine—it can be joy-filled and life-giving to sing the praises of God together. One of the most important things we do as a family is close every day in our home by singing the "Doxology." This simple Trinitarian hymn is a way for us to acknowledge as a family that every blessing or trial from the day is given from the hand of God, and He is worthy of our praise.

The Benefits of Singing

Singing is a spiritually beneficial practice for families. Matthew Henry echoes this when he says, "They that pray in the family do well; they that pray and read the Scriptures do better; but they that pray, and read, and sing do best of all."[7] From the time our children were two and three, I began writing Scripture songs for them. I saw how quickly they would learn things through music from the television shows they would watch. With this in mind, I wrote a Scripture song for every letter of the alphabet for us to teach our children Scripture and to hide God's Word in their heart.

Sing hymns; sing fun kids' songs.

Sing Scripture memory songs.

Conclusion

I was tired. At the time we had three children, and the days were full. Jamie and I had been praying through very important ministry decisions, and I was wrestling with fear. Our twin girls were also going through a stage when they were often fearful. In our family worship time, we had been regularly singing Psalm 56:3, "When I am afraid, I put my trust in you." One night, after repeated trips upstairs to help them and assure the girls they were fine, I told them it was quiet time, and there was to be no more talking. A few minutes later, they were at it again, and Avery was calling out for me again. As I walked to the top of the stairs to discipline them, I overheard Addy say, "Avery, don't be afraid; God is with us."

My heart sank to the floor. I began crying.

Rather than discipline them, I went into my study and marveled at the faithfulness of God. My three-year-old daughter led me in a meaningful time of worship.

If we have neglected worshipping God in our homes, we are often prone to feel condemnation and feel that we do not measure up as worship leaders. On the other hand, if we hold to a healthy practice of family worship, we are more prone to be filled with pride. Neither of these responses are appropriate. Realizing that in Christ we are fully accepted by the work of Jesus, not our own works, we are reminded of the amazing nature of grace.

Donald Whitney, in his wonderful treatment of family worship, exhorts those who have not successfully led their homes in family worship:

> Fathers, husbands—if you have been negligent in this duty and great privilege, repent by starting family worship today. Again, you may feel awkward about what to say to your wife or your children about starting, but simply say that God has convicted you of your responsibility to lead in family worship and you want to start at a given time today or tonight. Almost certainly your wife will be thrilled more than you can imagine to hear you say that. Your children may or may not be as enthusiastic, but that does not really matter. The less interested they are, the more your family needs family worship. The Lord will help you. He does not call His Spirit-begotten sons to this task without giving them the power of the Holy Spirit to accomplish it. The same Father who gave you the gospel and who drew you to Christ will strengthen you by His Spirit to put on this badge of godly manhood.[8]

We must realize that we don't pursue the practice of family worship to gain the approval of God. We practice worship in our homes because, in Christ, we have been given the approval of God. With this in mind, we marvel at the grace of God and desire for Him to be glorified in our homes. We hold out the gospel to our wives and children, praying that as we do, an environment of grace will mark our family.

Our ultimate aim is to point people to the true and better Worship Leader. It is Jesus who enables and perfects the worship of His people (1 Tim. 2:5; Heb. 2:12). My aim as a husband is not to be perfect, but to continually hold out the gospel to my wife. My aim as a father is not perfection, but to point my children to the true and better Father. My prayer for my family and yours is that we would bring glory to God by leading gospel-centered homes that practice the biblical scope of worship. May the theology of our homes lead to them be filled with joyful doxology.

Three Prayers

1. Pray that God would make your home a place where He is worshipped in your routine of life, and in times of regular family worship.

2. Pray for the father in your home (yourself, if applicable), that God would give him the faith and courage to lead and pastor your home.

3. Pray for the others in your church, that their homes would also be homes marked by peace, and filled with gospel-centered worship.

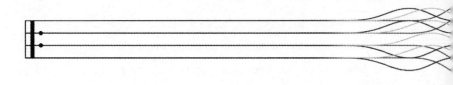

12

The Worship Leader and Singing

Matt Mason, The Church at Brook Hills (Birmingham, Alabama)

> *Oh come, let us sing to the LORD; let us make a joyful*
> *noise to the rock of our salvation! Let us come into his*
> *presence with thanksgiving; let us make a joyful noise*
> *to him with songs of praise! For the LORD is a great*
> *God, and a great King above all gods.*
>
> PSALM 95:1–3

Like every other Christian, my story is one in which I
look back and see that the grace of God has come at me
from a thousand directions. I remember when the Bible first

became illuminated before my eyes. The more I read—and this is still true—the more its truth sank deep, creating understanding, conviction, gratefulness, wonder. I could go on to speak of God engaging my heart during times of prayer, hearing the Word preached, or partaking of the Lord's Supper. Not to mention God's grace in creation and providence or, to be more specific, gifts like marriage and children. But even if I were to expand on each of these wonderful gifts, I can't adequately tell the story of God's grace in my life without coming to what the psalmist speaks of in Psalm 95: the grace that is known and experienced when God's people gather and lift their voices in songs of praise.

Singing and Seeing

I grew up in a small local church my dad planted in New Orleans. My mom played the Hammond B3 organ, which was the dominant instrument for gathered worship in the earlier years. We'd sing "Victory in Jesus," "Glorify Thy Name," "Blessed Assurance," and "The Blood Will Never Lose Its Power."

I stood next to Sister Melonda every Sunday. She sang the alto part from the first note to the last, which is how I first learned to sing harmony. It was a small but enthusiastic alto section right there on the second pew. Sometimes Dad would spontaneously invite her up and ask her to sing "His Eye Is on the Sparrow." Her tone was beautiful, her heart heavy. She would wipe her eyes as she sang. So would Dad.

I confess that as a child I did a lot of people watching during corporate worship. Brother Wayne was on my left. I studied him often. He wasn't the loudest singer in the room—that would've been Mr. Stan. But, often, his countenance was so full of joy I had to resist the urge to stare.

With time, gathered singing became less observation-oriented. I would stop and wonder what the words meant.

> *What can wash away my sins?*
> *Nothing but the blood of Jesus.*
> *What can make me whole again?*
> *Nothing but the blood of Jesus.*

As the seeds of the gospel began to yield greater understanding and love for Christ, I began to feel the truth and beauty of these words, and sang them with increasing exuberance . . .

> *Oh, precious is the flow*
> *That makes me white as snow*
> *No other fount I know*
> *Nothing but the blood of Jesus!*

I've met many believers who would share similar experiences of God's grace in the context of gathered singing. And it's no coincidence.

The Summons to Sing and the Promises of Grace

The Bible has a built-in hymnal, the book of Psalms, comprised of 150 songs, written over a period of about fifteen hundred years. These songs communicate truth about the character and the mighty deeds of the God of Israel. And these songs are responsive expressions of dependence on, reverence before, and delight in God.

There are more than five hundred references to singing in the Bible and more than fifty direct commands to sing.

Scripture couldn't be more clear. The God we worship delights in the sung praises of His people. But, we may ask, is this merely a sacred obligation? "Just do it because I said so"? Or are there promises of grace that accompany the summons to sing? Is God active during gathered singing? If so, what is He doing?

Sing . . . and See God's Holiness and Grace

We're not very far in the Psalms before we are met by a holy God who does not regard sin casually. Actually, the very first verse of Psalms speaks of the blessing that comes to the one who doesn't sit comfortably with sin. The God of

Psalm 1 is a God who judges the wicked, such that the last verse reads:

> For the LORD knows the way of the righ-
> teous, but the way of the wicked will perish. (v. 6)

Many of the songs in God's inspired hymnal expose the contrast between God's holiness and our sinfulness. David knew this well. He recognizes that he had sinned against God and that God would be perfectly right to condemn him.

> Against you, you only, have I sinned and
> done what is evil in your sight, so that you may
> be justified in your words and blameless in your
> judgment. (Ps. 51:4)

What does this all have to do with us? Though it's true that we find ourselves in a different chapter of redemptive history than David did as he wrote Psalm 51, we should remember that God's character doesn't change. These psalms remind us that David's God, and ours, is a God who hates sin. He is holy and pure in all of His ways (Pss. 30:4; 47:8; 77:13). And He calls us to be His holy people (Pss. 18:36; 24:4; 73:1).

Then how do we sing these kinds of truths in a way that reckons with the new covenant gospel reality? Consider for example Psalm 15:

O Lord, who shall sojourn in your tent?
Who shall dwell on your holy hill? (v. 1)

This tent is a reference to the Tabernacle. When the people of Israel were delivered from slavery in Egypt, they became a sojourning people. They followed the cloud by day and the pillar of fire by night. And when the cloud stopped, they knew, this is where we make camp tonight. And tents would be pitched for all the tribes of Israel—tents as far as the eye could see. And in the center of all the tribal tents was God's tent. And it was holy. If you were an Israelite, you didn't just saunter on into God's tent. It was a hallowed place of worship. It was the dwelling place of God.

This psalm asks who may draw near to the presence of a holy God. For the spiritually self-aware, the answer that comes next is not encouraging.

He who walks blamelessly and does what is
right and speaks truth in his heart. (Ps. 15:2)

It goes on to state the qualities of the one who may safely approach God's holy presence. This individual doesn't slander, but acts in love toward his neighbor, takes up no reproach against his friend, sides with God and the godly against the wicked. He or she doesn't break a promise even when it is costly, and is marked by integrity in business, finance, and personal dealings.

Psalm 24 asks a similar question and summarizes the answer this way: The one who may stand in God's holy place is "he who has clean hands and a pure heart" (v. 4).

This brings us back to the question of the gospel. How do we account for Psalms 15 and 24 in light of the new covenant and what Christ has accomplished for His people? Can't this end up taking us in a moralistic, clean-up-your-act direction?

Unfortunately, yes, that's possible. But songs that speak of God's holiness and our sin do not contradict the gospel. When effectively led and communicated, these themes shine light on the beauty of what God has accomplished in Christ.

Let's come to the New Testament then. The first part of the New Testament's response to Psalm 15's, "Who shall come into God's presence" is a boisterous, "Jesus Christ can!" *He* has clean hands and a pure heart. *He* has done no evil and broken no promise. *He* may sojourn in God's tent and stand in God's holy place. But the New Testament has more to say: Jesus Christ can come into God's holy presence *and all who are in Him (by faith alone) may enter as well.*

> We have this as a sure and steadfast anchor
> of the soul, a hope that enters into the inner
> place behind the curtain, where Jesus has gone
> as a forerunner *on our behalf,* having become
> a high priest forever. (Heb. 6:19–20, emphasis
> added)

Apart from being in Christ, God's tent is not a safe place for sinners. The Psalms gesture in both directions. They speak of the God before whom no sinner may stand (Ps. 1:5). And they speak of the God who has graciously made provision for His sinful people (Pss. 51:1–2; 130:3–4).

Local church singing should comprehend both of these categories, because in so doing, God's gathered people are reminded both of the gospel and of our need for that gospel. The irony is if all our songs are about God's kindness, nearness, and grace, forgiveness will cease to be glorious to us and grace will no longer seem amazing. We may start thinking, *Grace is what God does. Forgiveness is God's job. What's He going to do,* not *forgive me?*

We need songs that say things like:

> *Holy, holy, holy*
> *Though the darkness hide Thee*
> *Though the eye of sinful men*
> *Thy glories may not see*
> *Only Thou art holy*

And what is God doing as we sing songs filled with these truths? By His Spirit, He causes us to see His holiness and grace. He awakens our souls to stand in awe of Him. He brings the gospel home to our hearts so that we will boast in Christ alone.

Sing . . . and Be Assured of God's Nearness

There's an emotional range of praise in the Psalms that involves more than energetic thanksgiving. The Psalms are full of songs that express the pains of living in a fallen world. In fact, many scholars point out that there are more psalms borne out of a desperate cry for help than any other genre.

> I cry aloud to God, aloud to God, and he will hear me. In the day of my trouble I seek the Lord; in the night my hand is stretched out without wearying; my soul refuses to be comforted. When I remember God, I moan; when I meditate, my spirit faints. Selah You hold my eyelids open; I am so troubled that I cannot speak. I consider the days of old, the years long ago. I said, "Let me remember my song in the night; let me meditate in my heart." Then my spirit made a diligent search. (Ps. 77:1–6)

We and the congregations we serve need to sing songs that remind us, in the dark night of the soul, that God is with us. He is a "very present help in time of trouble" (46:1). I would guess that that expression is one of the most oft-quoted statements in the Psalms. If that's true, the reason that verse is so dear is obvious. We feel the pains of life in a fallen world.

We feel not only moral evil but also the circumstantial evil that arises from it. The thorns and thistles, the pains in childbirth, the epileptic children, the barren woman. In a word, the evidences of Romans 8:20 that indeed the world has been "subjected to futility."

And the churches we long to serve are full of people who gather on any given Sunday, who come into the gathering feeling like their hearts are being ripped apart and their faith is wavering. And they wonder, *Has God forsaken me? Will He never again be favorable?*

Bob Kauflin has been a mentor to me for more than ten years and that relationship, wonderfully, also brings with it many expressions of care and friendship. Bob often urges worship leaders to see corporate worship as a context for pastoral care. We are not just singing songs. Our desire in worship planning is to pray and plan toward the goal of seeing God's Word brought home by the Holy Spirit to the hearts of those who are gathered. Our planning should be deeply pastoral in nature. We should be thinking about whether those who are battling for joy will have the opportunity to be strengthened by biblical truth through these songs.

When our daughter was four years old, she would commonly have outbreaks of sadness (read: meltdowns). She would often go into her room and sing mournful-sounding songs about what made her sad ("they won't let me have more ice cream"). She was a little blues singer.

The Psalms know how to sing the blues:

> I would like to make just one observation: the psalms, the Bible's own hymnbook, have almost entirely dropped from view in the contemporary Western evangelical scene. I am not certain about why this should be, but I have an instinctive feel that it has more than a little to do with the fact that a high proportion of the psalter is taken up with lamentation, with feeling sad, unhappy, tormented, and broken. In modern Western culture, these are simply not emotions which have much credibility: sure, people still feel these things, but to admit that they are a normal part of one's everyday life is tantamount to admitting that one has failed in today's health, wealth, and happiness society. . . . Few Christians in areas where the church has been strongest over recent decades—China, Africa, Eastern Europe—would regard uninterrupted emotional highs as normal Christian experience.[1]

Contrary to the popularity of hyper-faith teaching, it is possible to sing, and to live, with deep feelings of sorrow in our hearts and yet *not* be faithless or hopeless.

When we're reading something as emotionally dark as Psalm 38, how do we know the psalmist still has faith in God and hasn't given in to despair? In a real sense, the presence of the next verse, and the next verse, tells the story. The song continues. And though there doesn't seem to be an emotional lift or circumstantial "breakthrough" anywhere in the text, the last verse of the psalm is a prayer and a statement of Godward trust.

> Make haste to help me, O Lord, my salva-
> tion! (Ps. 38:22)

When we're truly faithless and hopeless we stop singing altogether. We stop praying. We quit. But the Godward song signals to us we are not giving into despair. We have a song to sing. To borrow a phrase from Psalm 77, we have a song in the night:

> *My life flows on in endless song,*
> *above earth's lamentation,*
> *I hear the sweet tho' far off hymn*
> *that hails a new creation.*
> *Thro' all the tumult and the strife*
> *I hear the music ringing*
> *It finds an echo in my soul.*
> *How can I keep from singing?*

What tho' my joys and comforts die?
The Lord my Savior liveth.
What tho' the darkness gather round?
Songs in the night he giveth.
No storm can shake my inmost calm
while to that refuge clinging.
Since Christ is Lord of heaven and earth
how can I keep from singing?[2]

What is God doing as we sing songs filled with these truths? By His Spirit, He is reminding us that He is not only Creator and King, but Comforter and Refuge. He is not only transcendent. He is immanent. He is giving hope through His Word to weary saints.

Sing . . . and Hear the Singer

As believers we've all experienced those wonderful moments in which God brings truth home to our hearts as we sing on Sunday morning. Suddenly we have a renewed sense of the majesty and greatness of God. There's almost a palpable urge to bow. Or perhaps we feel again the joy of sins forgiven. We want to shout, maybe even dance. Or in a season of hardship, we sense the nearness of God and are reminded that He loves us and will never leave us. The storms of circumstances are still a reality but we feel anchored. We believe we will see the goodness of the Lord in the land of the living, so we don't lose heart (Ps. 27:13).

These are gifts of grace and our God gives them generously. But there's something else God is doing as we gather to sing His praises. And this may come as a surprise.

> For it was fitting that he, for whom and
> by whom all things exist, in bringing many
> sons to glory, should make the founder of their
> salvation perfect through suffering. For he who
> sanctifies and those who are sanctified all have
> one source. That is why he is not ashamed to
> call them brothers, saying, "I will tell of your
> name to my brothers; in the midst of the con-
> gregation I will sing your praise. (Heb. 2:10–12)

This passage is drawn from Psalm 22, yet these words are attributed more ultimately to Jesus Himself. *Jesus* is saying, "I will tell of Your name to My brothers; in the midst of the congregation I will sing Your praise."

Here we realize that the ultimate worship Leader in the gathering, who enables us to know the Father—He tells us the Father's name—and who leads our song of adoration, is Christ Himself! We aren't the only ones singing. The church sings to a singing God.

> The Lord your God is in your midst, a
> mighty one who will save; he will rejoice over
> you with gladness; he will quiet you by his

love; he will exult over you with loud singing.
(Zeph. 3:17)

> It's only when we understand his [Christ's]
> presence in the church as being the fulfillment
> of God's promise in Zephaniah 3:17 (NIV) to
> "quiet you with his love" and "rejoice over you
> with singing" that a crucial aspect of our salva-
> tion comes into perspective. Jesus didn't coldly
> settle accounts for us. He doesn't bark us into
> improving ourselves. He unites us to himself
> in the glorious communion he has enjoyed for
> eternity with his heavenly Father. He resides
> within us to heal the broken places and reflesh
> our cauterized hearts. He sings us into a new
> mode of existence.[3]

The Father sings over us. The Son leads us into God's
tent to exalt the Father. And when the Spirit freshly fills His
gathered people in Ephesians 5:19, songs come out.

Listen for it next Sunday. As you join your congregation
in rehearsing the life-changing, humbling, joy-producing,
assurance-bringing truths of the gospel, listen for the Singer
who delights in His gathered people. When we're aware of
this reality, Sunday morning becomes anything but routine
or mundane. The alarm clock goes off, and our hearts begin
to say,

Oh come, let us sing to the Lord; let us make a joyful noise to the rock of our salvation! Let us come into his presence with thanksgiving; let us make a joyful noise to him with songs of praise! For the Lord is a great God, and a great King above all gods. (Ps. 95:1–3)

13

The Worship Leader
and the Gospel

*Ken Boer, Covenant Life Church
(Gaithersburg, Maryland)*

*Now I would remind you, brothers, of the gospel I
preached to you, which you received, in which you stand,
and by which you are being saved. . . . For I delivered
to you as of first importance what I also received: that
Christ died for our sins in accordance with the Scriptures, that he was buried, that he was raised on the
third day in accordance with the Scriptures, and that he
appeared to Cephas, then to the twelve.*

1 CORINTHIANS 15:1–5

You've made it to the last chapter. I hope that what you have read so far has both encouraged and challenged you in your role as a worship leader. In this final installment, I want to draw your attention back to the reason your church exists, the reason most of your songs exist, and—to put it bluntly—the reason you're not in hell right now.

That reason is the gospel—the good news that "Christ Jesus came into the world to save sinners" (1 Tim. 1:15). This is the best news that we could ever hear. It's more important than anything else that's been on your mind today. It's more important than any technique or idea you may have learned from this book. And it's most important for the people you lead.

The gospel is the power of God for salvation. Like the apostle Paul, we want to boast in the cross of Christ alone (Gal. 6:14). Just as heaven is filled with praises to Christ, so we, too, were made to join our voices in the endless praise of the Lamb who was slain (Rev. 5:9–14). This is the news upon which our entire ministry is built, so it's worth spending a little time reviewing.

What the Gospel Is

If you had to state the gospel in a few words, what would it be? How would you boil down the main message of the Bible? Four words that I've found helpful are *God,*

Man, Christ, and *Response.*[1] *God* existed before anything else existed and He created us. He is holy and perfect in all His attributes—His wisdom, justice, mercy, and love. God made *man* to glorify God, but instead of glorifying Him, humans disobeyed God and lived for their own glory. Humanity's rebellion against God makes them deserving of God's eternal condemnation. God sent *Christ*, His Son, to take on human flesh, live a perfect life, and receive the wrath humankind deserved. God raised Christ from the dead and seated Him at His right hand, and God offers forgiveness of sins and eternal life to any whose *response* consists of repentance of their sins and trust in Jesus as their only hope of salvation.

The implications of this gospel are innumerable. They extend from the minutiae of our everyday lives to the future of the entire cosmos. When we sin, we don't need to fear condemnation, because Christ has already been condemned for us. When we're not measuring up to expectations, we don't need to prove ourselves, because Someone else already did everything right for us. When the circumstances of our lives change, we know that through Jesus, God will cause everything to work together for our good. We can be eternally optimistic because we know the end of the story.

When the gospel sinks deep into our hearts, everything begins to change. We begin to realize that the good news affects everything, and it feels like we're seeing the world for the first time. It's as if someone just turned the lights on. Our job as worship leaders is to help people see the gospel more clearly and understand how it affects everything. Let's now look at some of the ways we can make our leadership more gospel-centered, so that the people we lead will become more aware of what He's done and bring Him even greater praise.

Let the Gospel Affect Your Heart

Worship Leader. What a title. Sometimes I wish we could get rid of it. When you realize worship is more than singing or what occurs in a church meeting, leading others in worship becomes a far higher calling. Every day, through my words and actions, I am constantly encouraging other people to worship along with me. I don't even have to sing to do it. I constantly tell people what I treasure, what I believe is most enjoyable, and what truly matters in this life. The only problem is that the object of my worship isn't always God. Sometimes I feel like the football player who picks up a fumble, runs hard, and hears the crowd roar, only to realize he's in the wrong end zone.

God made you and me to be worshippers. We're constantly pouring out worship. We can't *not* worship. The objects of our worship are whatever we love, trust, and praise the most. Sadly, these are often money, sex, comfort, or people's approval instead of God. We've exchanged the glory of God for created things (Rom. 1:18–23).

But the good news is that God hasn't left us there. If we've trusted in Christ, we have been forgiven for our false worship. God has put His Spirit in our hearts so that through His Son we can worship in the way that pleases Him. And though we don't always worship Him perfectly, our every moment of false worship is covered by the blood of the only man whose worship was perfect—Jesus. When we worship God, we experience the joy we were meant to experience all along because we're doing what we were created to do.

One sin that plagues worship leaders is pride. I mean, shouldn't the church be grateful to us for all the ways we help them worship God? We'd never say so out loud, but deep down we really want people to think we're awesome, like God.

Some of us, though, have the opposite problem. We don't think we're very good, and we're afraid people are going to actually realize we're not. That problem, sometimes called "the fear of man," is actually the flip side of pride. Whether you think you're doing well or think you're doing poorly, your driving concern is still what people think of you.

How do we apply the gospel to our pride as worship leaders? A good place to start is to remember people probably aren't thinking about us nearly as much as we think they are. More important, we need to remember that others aren't created to worship us but to worship God! Trying to become the object of their worship is making ourselves an idol. For this we need to repent and ask for forgiveness, just like we need to do the same for all of the other idolatry in our lives.

Whether people say good or bad about us, we can remember that the judgment others make about us will never be worse than what the cross has already said about us.[2] But they can't condemn us either, for it is God who condemns and justifies (Rom. 8:33–34). He's already counted us righteous, and nothing can change that (2 Cor. 5:21). We don't have to search for acceptance because we've already found our ultimate identity in Christ (Col. 3:3), and we've been made dearly loved children of God (1 John 3:1). The gospel has pride-killing power that frees our hearts to worship Him alone.

Choose Great Songs

Let's transition now to planning your service. One of the best places you can start is by simply finding songs rich in content about what Christ has done and how it applies to our lives. If you build a repertoire of great songs, it makes your planning each week much easier. Regardless of what you choose, you can know you are feeding your congregation the riches of the gospel. This is not to say that you should take planning lightly. You can spend hours and hours practicing your songs and transitions, but your practice will usually only be as helpful as your songs are.

Songs are a way of teaching one another (Col. 3:16). For that reason, don't base your choices on popularity or the latest hits, but choose songs based on what will feed people's souls. Choose songs that talk about heaven and hell, about wrath and mercy, about God's glory and the fact that He changes lives. Lean toward songs that are specific and avoid songs that are vague. Don't pick songs that you could sing to Allah or to your wife and they would still make just as much sense. Make sure they're specific about the Father and the Son and the Spirit. Don't develop a repertoire of songs that describes sin as shame and brokenness but fails to mention it's also an offense against God deserving judgment. Choose songs that show the depths of sin and judgment that, by contrast, make the heights of God's love appear even greater. Don't force your people to work through a fog of unnecessarily hard language or complex music to see Jesus. Each song doesn't have to cover as much ground as the book of Romans.

On the flip side, some leaders (myself included) have believed that to be gospel-centered, every song we sing has to explicitly state the gospel, or more narrowly, substitutionary atonement. But we shouldn't be more gospel-centered than the Bible is. The Bible includes all kinds of topics, and our services and songs should address the full range of human experience.

If the history of the universe is a movie, Christ's death and resurrection is the turning point of the movie. Don't let people grow dull by *only* ever playing the highlight reel. Let them see the whole movie! At the same time, don't be ashamed of going to the highlights again and again, because without them the rest of the movie doesn't make sense.

Make Gospel Connections

Part of our job as worship leaders is to help people make connections between the gospel and their lives. Here is an illustration of how I think about these connections:[3]

Figure 1

In the center (we'll call it circle 1) is the gospel—the good news that Christ died for our sins. In the next circle out (circle 2) are the implications of the gospel—biblical doctrine that flows from the fact that Christ died for us. Finally, in the outer circle (circle 3) are the applications for our lives—our hopes, our desires, and our fears. It's where we live every day. God desires that these three circles be connected in the way we think, talk, and live because the gospel is meant to change our lives. Let me use Galatians 4:4–7 to illustrate:

> God sent forth his Son, born of woman, born
> under the law, to redeem those who were under
> the law, so that we might receive adoption as
> sons. And because you are sons, God has sent the
> Spirit of his Son into our hearts, crying, "Abba!
> Father!" So you are no longer a slave, but a son,
> and if a son, then an heir through God.

The good news (circle 1) is that God sent His Son to redeem those under the law. The implication (circle 2) is we are no longer slaves, but God's precious children who have His Spirit in our hearts. Because of this, we can cry out to God as our Abba Father and find help from Him (circle 3). Another example is 1 Corinthians 6:19–20: "You are not your own, for you were bought with a price. So glorify God in your body." God bought us with a price (circle 1), which means that we're no longer our own but His (circle 2), and are to honor Him in our daily lives (circle 3).

We help people grow in the gospel by making these connections. This is what gospel-centered pastors do in their preaching, and what the best biblical counselors do when they are helping an individual one-on-one. If someone coming into your service is discouraged because they've lost their job, it's not enough just to say, "Believe the gospel." While we should direct them to the gospel, it's far more helpful to show them the *specific ways* in which the gospel applies to their circumstances. We can remind the person who lost their job that *because* (1) God did not spare His own Son but gave Him for us all, (2) it is a small thing for Him to provide us with all things, (3) including our basic necessities (Rom. 8:32). We also know that (1) for those who love God and are called by Him, (2) He will cause all things to work together for our good, (3) even the loss of a job (Rom. 8:28).

What does this look like for a worship leader? It means, both in your planning and as you actually lead in the service, you are constantly thinking back and forth between the circles. If you are verbally introducing a song that contains the gospel and some implications, make mention of how this specifically applies to our lives. Often it can be introduced with a simple "if": "If you feel condemned for your sin today . . ." or "If God seems distant to you . . ."

When you pray, let the content of your prayer contain both what Christ has done and what it means for our hearts. When you're choosing a song to connect with a sermon, think through *how* the gospel connects with the message's application, and let it drive what you say and the songs you pick (hopefully your pastor is making these connections as well). You'll find that certain songs do a better job than others in showing the implications of the gospel. One of the reasons "In Christ Alone" is such a great song is because it makes these connections.

> [A]s he stands in victory,
> sin's curse has lost its grip on me,
> for I am his and he is mine,
> bought with the precious blood of Christ.
> No guilt in life, no fear in death—
> This is the pow'r of Christ in me.[4]

Find ways to remind people of what the gospel means for Monday morning. Our lives change when we apply the gospel not just to Sundays or to the major moments of our lives, but to our everyday moments. Make these connections, for they will help the people you lead more fully offer their lives as worship.

Order Your Service to Reflect the Gospel

Another way you can help your people dwell in the riches of the gospel is by ordering your service in a way that reflects the gospel.[5] Your church may follow a formal liturgy, or like mine, you may not have a formal order every week. But even those of us who don't have an official liturgy still have one, because every church has a normal order of doing things. It's not a question of whether you have a liturgy; it's whether you plan yours well.

It's important for us to learn from the ways Christians throughout history have ordered their services. The best historic liturgies have reflected the pattern of the gospel in their structure to ensure God's people are interacting with Him around the main features of the gospel each week. If the main elements of the gospel are *God, Man, Christ,* and *Response*, consider how a service order could follow this pattern.

- *God*: The service begins with a call to worship God and a Scripture or song that tells of His greatness and glory.
- *Man*: In light of who God is, we recognize how far we have fallen short of His glory, and we confess our sin.

- *Christ*: We remind ourselves of Christ's work on our behalf, and we offer praise and thanksgiving to God for His mercy. We listen to the Word to grow in knowing the God who has saved us.

- *Response:* The Word also tells us about God's purposes for our lives. We offer prayers asking that He would cause His kingdom to come and that He would meet our needs. We give financially to see this news spread. And in case anyone missed it, we repeat the story of *Christ*'s death to save *Man* from *God*'s wrath through the meal He gave us by observing communion. The service concludes on a note of *Response* as we are sent as God's people to proclaim this good news.

The whole structure is built with the intention of weekly rehearsing the major elements of the gospel. The Bible doesn't say that we have to put our services together in a particular order. But there are things we can learn from Christians in the past and from the logic of the gospel. It makes sense to call people to live lives of holiness *after* they've been made aware of the mercy of God. It makes sense to confess sin *in light of* God's holiness. Thanksgiving for mercy is even sweeter after we acknowledge our need for it.

Let this flow of thought influence the way you plan. You don't have to follow the order strictly, but sometimes putting things in this order helps people become more aware of how the pieces of the gospel fit together. To push yourself outside of just picking songs, it can be helpful to plan what you want to accomplish (exalting God's glory, confessing sin, etc.) and *then* choose which forms you want to use (songs, prayer, Scripture, etc.). You'll find that many of the best songs actually wrap all these elements into one, and you can use them almost anywhere in the service.

You can use the words *God, Man, Christ,* and *Response* as a checklist to make sure you're telling the story each week. Does your plan for this Sunday include God's glory, our need for forgiveness, God's mercy through Jesus, and the call of faith? What are you feeding your people weekly? How will you ensure that you highlight these aspects of the gospel regularly and consistently? Whatever you do, make sure you are helping your people weekly rehearse and celebrate the good news of God's grace.

Wear Your Heart on Your Sleeve

One other way that you can help your people be moved by the gospel is by being moved by the gospel yourself. It's not sufficient to merely proclaim truth about God. Truth is meant to inspire awe, repentance, faith, and joy within our hearts. As Bob Kauflin expresses it, "Magnifying God's greatness *begins* with the proclamation of objective, biblical truths about God, but it *ends* with the expression of deep and holy affection toward God."[6]

We have strong emotions about many different areas in our lives—relationships, work, politics, music, and the list goes on. But our strongest and deepest emotions should come in relation to the gospel. Nothing should create greater awe in our hearts than God's glory. Nothing should horrify us more than the depth of our sin. Nothing should be as shocking and amazing as the cross, and nothing should give us more joy than knowing we're forgiven. The sheer number of emotions that are commended and commanded of believers throughout the Bible is staggering.[7]

If we want to cultivate godly emotion in the people we lead, we need to start with ourselves. Begin by praying God will give us appropriate heart-attitudes toward the gospel, for while much of what we do is taught and planned, a good deal of it is learned by intuition. If our hearts are affected by what God has done, it is going to come out in the way we speak (Prov. 4:23). It's going to come out in our physical expression, whether it's simply through our face (Ps. 34:5) or with our hands and feet (Pss. 47:1; 149:3). It doesn't look the same for all of us, because God made us each unique. Spirituality can't be measured by mere outward expression.

But if there is an inward reality, there is going to be some degree of outward expression, no matter how small.

People need to sense that when we meet together we believe that we really are meeting with the living God. They need to sense that we're not as excited about the logistics of the service or the music or the preacher as we are about the Savior of the world. They need to sense that we actually believe heaven and hell are real. They need those who stand in front of them to lead with tears in their eyes and pleas for repentance. They need worship leaders who will sing their guts out because they "rejoice with joy that is inexpressible and filled with glory," knowing they will obtain the outcome of their faith, the salvation of their souls (1 Pet. 1:8).

Love Jesus. And don't be afraid to show people that you love Him. It will help them love Him more.

Faithfulness: As you think about how to serve your church, sometimes it helps to think about what's going to matter ten thousand years from now. It's probably going to be a little different from what seems important today. After you spend countless ages beholding the glory of God in endless joy, you're probably not going to care whether you had the best lighting, the most talented band, or the best voice. You're not going to care whether the album you recorded went gold or was only heard by your mom and a few close friends. You're not going to care how big of a ministry position God gave you. In fact, you'll probably feel He gave you more than enough responsibility! But a few things will matter, like whether the people who walked through the doors of your church heard the gospel and if you lived your life with faith. And you'll be able to praise God for Jesus' blood that covers all your failings.

On the final day you're never going to hear, "Well done, great musician." God doesn't use the same standards we do. Instead, pray for help and faithfully invest the talents and resources He's given you, so that in the end you will hear:

> "Well done, good and faithful servant. You
> have been faithful over a little; I will set you
> over much. Enter into the joy of your master."
> (Matt. 25:21)

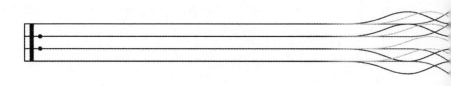

NOTES

Introduction

1. C. S. Lewis, *Mere Christianity* (San Francisco: Harper/ Zondervan, 1947), 153.

Chapter 1

1. R. Scott Clark and Joel E. Kim, eds., *Always Reformed: Essays in Honor of W. Robert Godfrey* (California: Westminster Seminary, 2012), 116–34.

2. *Works of Jonathan Edwards, Volume 16, Letters and Personal Writings*, ed. George S. Claghorn (New Haven: Yale University Press, 1957), 755.

3. Al Mohler, "The Reformation We Need Today," Panel Discussion with Ligon Duncan, Mark Dever, and John MacArthur from the Together for the Gospel Conference in Louisville, Kentucky, 2016. Video available at http://www.doxologyandtheology.com/blog/post/t4g.

4. Mark Dever and Paul Alexander, *The Deliberate Church: Building Your Ministry on the Gospel* (Wheaton, IL: Crossway, 2005).

5. John Piper, *Think: The Life of the Mind and the Love of God* (Wheaton, IL: Crossway, 2011), 15.

6. Isaac Watts et al., *The Psalms and Hymns of Dr. Watts, Arranged by Dr. Rippon: With Dr. Rippon's Selection: in One Volume; with Improved Indexes* (Philadelphia, PA: David Clark, 1927), 555.

7. John Piper, Online Interview, http://www.desiringgod.org/ interviews/what-do-truth-and-praise-have-to-do-with-each-other.

8. Harold M. Best, *Dumbfounded Praying* (Eugene, OR: Wipf and Stock Publications, 2011), 108.

9. Thomas Brooks, *The Select Works of Thomas Brooks* (1824), 190.

10. Anne Steele, *The Works of Mrs. Anne Steele, Complete in Two Volumes: Comprehending Poems on Subjects Chiefly Devotional; and Miscellaneous Pieces in Prose and Verse; Heretofore Published under the Title of Theodosia* (Boston: Printed and published by Munroe, Francis and Parker, 1808).

Chapter 2

1. "All Hail the Power of Jesus' Name," by Edward Perronet and Oliver Holden.

2. John Piper, *Desiring God* (Colorado Springs: Multnomah, 2001), 81.

3. "Then Samuel took a stone and set it up between Mizpah and Shen and called its name Ebenezer; for he said, 'Till now the LORD has helped us.'"

4. "Behold, I have engraved you on the palms of my hands; your walls are continually before me."

5. See Exodus 12:27; Job 1:20; and Psalm 95:6.

6. John Piper, *Brothers, We Are Not Professionals* (Nashville: B&H Publishing Group, 2002), 3–4.

Chapter 3

1. See esp. James B. Torrance, *Worship, Community, and the Triune God of Grace* (Downers Grove: InterVarsity Press, 1996), 43–67.

2. Revelation 4–5 and other passages highlight the equal worship of Father and Son. Less obvious in Scripture is the worship of the Spirit, but passages that come close (e.g., John 4:24) alongside the scriptural commands to basically "worship God" strongly press us to give the Spirit direct praise.

3. "The redemptive flow of biblical worship inevitably makes our liturgy Christ-centered. This does not mean that Christian worship diminishes the honor of any other member of the Trinity. God the

Father makes our worship Christ-centered by redeeming us through the work of his Son, and giving the Spirit to testify of him. Because worship is a response to this witness of redemption, the grace God provides through his Son is the thread that sews the service together" (Bryan Chapell, *Christ-Centered Worship: Letting the Gospel Shape Our Practice* [Grand Rapids: Baker, 2009], 113).

4. "In our worship the Holy Spirit comes forth from God, uniting us to the response and obedience and faith and prayer of Jesus, and returns to God, raising us up in Jesus to participate in the worship of heaven and in the eternal communion of the Holy Trinity" (T. F. Torrance, *Theology in Reconstruction* [Grand Rapids: Eerdmans, 1965], 250, qtd. in John Witvliet, "The Trinitarian DNA of Christian Worship: Perennial Themes in Recent Theological Literature," Yale Institute of Sacred Music *Colloquium Journal,* http://www.yale.edu/ism/colloq_journal /vol2/witvliet1.html, accessed February 27, 2012).

5. Cf. Simon Chan, *Liturgical Theology* (Downers Grove: InterVarsity Press, 2006), 161.

6. Lester Ruth, "How Great Is Our God: The Trinity in Contemporary Worship Music," in *The Message in the Music: Studying Contemporary Praise & Worship,* Robert Woods and Brian Walrath, eds. (Nashville: Abingdon, 2007), 29–42; James B. Torrance, *Worship,* 19–24.

7. This observation is made by John Witvliet ("Trinitarian DNA").

8. "[The doctrine of the Trinity] ensures that both the content of Christian proclamation and the source for perceiving that content are not less than God" (John Witvliet, "Trinitarian DNA").

9. Matt Redman, "Gifted Response," ©2004 Thank You Music, admin. by worshiptogether.com songs; cf. Robin Parry, *Worshipping Trinity: Coming Back to the Heart of Worship* (Eugene: Wipf & Stock: 2005), 88.

10. Cf. Fred Sanders, *The Deep Things of God: How the Trinity Changes Everything* (Wheaton: Crossway, 2010), 98.

11. For a thorough biblical treatment of the historicity and ecumenicity of gospel-shaped worship, see Bryan Chapell, *Christ-Centered*

Worship: Letting the Gospel Shape Our Practice (Grand Rapids: Baker, 2009).

12. I wonder whether songwriter Joel Houston hasn't come awfully close to this very thing in his song "Father," whose chorus sings, "Father / let heaven and earth collide in the endless wonder / of Your love upon the cross" (©2010 Hillsong Music Publishing [admin by EMI Christian Music Publishing]).

13. "Christian preaching cannot therefore be understood apart from the doctrine of the Trinity: on the basis of the past work of His Son, and in the perspective of the work He is yet to do, God the father gives us today, through the Holy Spirit, faith in the salvation which has been accomplished and hope in the salvation yet to be revealed" (Jean-Jacques von Allmen, *Preaching and Congregation* [Richmond: John Knox Press, 1962], 8, qtd. in Witvliet, "Trinitarian DNA").

Chapter 4

1. C. S. Lewis, *Reflections in the Psalms* (New York: Mariner Books, 1958), paraphrased from pp. 90–98.

2. Dissertation by Jonathan Edwards, "The End of Which God Created the World," 1765.

3. Missionary story told to contributor.

Chapter 5

1. Carl Olof Cederlund, *Vasa I: The Archaeology of a Swedish Warship of 1628*, Frederick M. Hocker, ed. (Sweden: Medstroms Bokforlag, 2011).

Chapter 6

1. Thomas Merton, *No Man Is an Island* (New York: Mariner Books, 2002).

2. Arthur Bennett, ed., *Valley of Vision* (UK: Banner of Truth, 1975).

Chapter 7

1. Bryan Chapell, *Christ-Centered Worship* (Grand Rapids: Baker, 2005).

2. Material taken from Professor Mike Farley at Covenant Seminary.

3. Tim Keller, *Paul's Letters to the Galatians: Living in Line with the Truth of the Gospel* (New York: Redeemer Presbyterian Church, 2003), 2.

4. See http://cardiphonia.org/2012/01/19/observations-on-the-new-hymns-movement-part-2.

Chapter 8

1. Michael Card, *Scribbling in the Sand* (Westmont, IL: InterVarsity Press, 2004), 86.

Chapter 9

1. For a wonderful treatment of this topic, see *Desiring the Kingdom* by James K. A. Smith.

Chapter 11

1. Jonathan Edwards, "Farewell Sermon," *The Works of Jonathan Edwards, Vol. 1* (Carlisle: Banner of Truth), 206.

2. Joel Beeke, *Family Worship* (Grand Rapids: Reformation Heritage, 2002, 2009).

3. See *Jesus Storybook Bible* by Sally Lloyd Jones, *The Big Picture Bible*, and *The Gospel Project* curriculum.

4. Thomas Watson, James Nichols, eds., *Puritan Sermons, 1659–1689,* Vol. 2 (Wheaton: Richard Owens Roberts, reprint 1981), 62.

5. Charles Spurgeon, "Restraining Prayer," *Metropolitan Tabernacle Pulpit*, Vol. 51, 327.

6. John Newton, *John Newton's Letters: Family Worship,* Vol. 1, Letter IV.

7. Spoken by Matthew Henry in *The Happy Duty of Daily Praise* by C. H. Spurgeon (1877).

8. Donald S. Whitney, *Family Worship* (Shepherdsville, KY: The Center for Biblical Spirituality, 2006), 26.

Chapter 12

1. Carl Trueman, *Wages of Sin* (Denver: Mentor, 2005), 158–59.

2. See http://www.hymnsite.com/fws/hymn.cgi?2212.

3. Reggie Kidd, *With One Voice: Discovering Christ's Song in Our Worship* (Grand Rapids: Baker Books, 2005), 109.

Chapter 13

1. Greg Gilbert, *What Is the Gospel?* (Wheaton: Crossway, 2010).

2. Alfred Poirier, "The Cross and Criticism," *Journal of Biblical Counseling* 17, no. 3 (Spring 1999): 16–20.

3. This is drawn and adapted from Mike Bullmore, "Gospel Implications," http://www.9marks.org/journal/gospel-implications (accessed October 15, 2012).

4. Stuart Townend and Keith Getty, "In Christ Alone" (Kingsway, 2001).

5. Bryan Chapell, *Christ-Centered Worship* (Grand Rapids: Baker Academic, 2009) offers a fuller (and very helpful) explanation of this approach. I am using simpler categories.

6. Bob Kauflin, *Worship Matters* (Wheaton, IL: Crossway Books, 2008), 65.

7. Jonathan Edwards, *The Religious Affections* (Carlisle, PA: Banner of Truth, 1961), 21–48.